Y0-BUT-501

IN THE MIDST
OF
THE WORLD

A Call To Holiness

In every walk of life, the Christian may attain to holiness by this simple, but sublime spirituality of

ST. FRANCIS DE SALES

IN THE MIDST
OF
THE WORLD

A Call To Holiness

THE SPIRITUAL DIRECTORY OF
ST. FRANCIS DE SALES

Translated from the German

Selections from the Writings of the Saint
Compiled and Edited
and Explanatory Commentaries Written

by
Sister Joanna Marie Wenzel, V.H.M.

Assisted by
Sister Aimee Franklin, V.H.M.

Illustrations by
Sister Judith Ann Shea, C.S.J.

PUBLISHED BY
SISTERS OF THE VISITATION
Ridge Boulevard at 89th Street   Brooklyn, NY 11209

Nihil Obstat: Reverend John Brown, S.T.L.
Delegated Censor

Imprimatur: ✠ Francis J. Mugavero
Bishop of Brooklyn

Brooklyn, New York
July 3, 1985

Library of Congress Catalog Card No. 85-090422

Copyright © 1985 by the Sisters of the Visitation, Brooklyn, NY

All rights reserved. This book may not be reproduced in whole or in part, for any purposes whatever without permission from the Publisher.

Any information regarding this book may be addressed to: Sisters of the Visitation, Ridge Boulevard at 89th Street, Brooklyn, NY 11209

Dedication

For the glory of the Heart of God -

that the hearts of many
may respond to Him in deep love
through the message of these pages.

For the vast majority of Christians seeking a holy way of living, the path will be found amid the simple and ordinary features of life.

Life, with its joys and sorrows, its burdens and responsibilities, its times of quiet beauty and fearful disappointments, contains the essential ingredients for living a life in union with almighty God.

Francis de Sales was a person who recognized the great potential for holiness amid the busyness of the world. He developed an approach to holiness for himself and, in a spirit of generosity and compassion, sought to share that approach with others.

The reader will find in these pages the living spirit of this gentle, practical saint which, transcending the passing of time, speaks to the always contemporary problem facing believers: How to achieve holiness in the midst of the world. The reader will also find here the underlying conviction of Francis which runs through his thoughts and, indeed, his life -that sanctity is both desirable and possible.

Francis J. Mugavero, D.D.
Bishop of Brooklyn

March 25, 1984
Feast of the Annunciation of Our Lady

CONTENTS

PREFACE.. xiii

A WORD OF ADVICE..................................... xv

ACKNOWLEDGMENTS xvii

ORIGIN OF THE SPIRITUAL DIRECTORY xix

HOW TO PRACTICE THE SPIRITUAL DIRECTORY,
    "IN THE MIDST OF THE WORLD" xxi

JACOB'S LADDER xxiii

PART I

THE SPIRITUAL DIRECTORY
AND
COMMENTARIES

1. FAITHFULNESS IN ALL THINGS
    - The Great Intention 4
    - How to Apply Our Works More Particularly
        to the Love of God 5
    - Commentary on the "Great Intention" 6
    - Direction of Intention 8
    - The Value of Small Actions 9
    - Commentary on "Direction of Intention".................. 10

2. PRAYER
    - Prayer 16
    - The Necessity of Prayer 17
    - Meditation 18
    - Preparation for Meditation 19
    - Commentary on "Prayer" 20
    - Prayer of Praise... 23
    - Contemplation and How to Prepare for It 25

3. PRAYER OF THE HEART THROUGHOUT THE DAY
    - Preparation for the Day-Morning Exercise 28
    - How We Should Receive Inspirations........................ 29
    - Quiet Interval with the Lord 30
    - Night Prayer-Examination of Conscience 30
    - How We Should Carry Out Inspirations 31
    - Atmosphere of Spiritual Retreat 32
    - Living in God's Presence....................................... 33
    - Aspirations and Ejaculatory Prayers
        (Short Prayers and Scripture Phrases) 36
    - The Use of Aspirations 38

4. SACRAMENTS AND THE WORD OF GOD
  - Sacrament of Reconciliation 40
  - Reconciliation 41
  - Eucharistic Mystery - Communion 42
  - Greatness of the Eucharistic Mystery 43
  - The Word of God and Spiritual Reading 44
  - Importance of the Word of God and
        Spiritual Reading 45

5. LIFE IN THE PRESENCE OF GOD
  - The Sea Swallows 48
  - Care and Diligence in Managing Our Affairs 49
  - Occupations and State in Life 52
  - Faithfulness in All Things 53
  - To Become All Things to All 56
  - The Measure of Love of Neighbor 57
  - Commentary on Measure of Love of Neighbor 59
  - Strive After Peace 62
  - Crosses 63
  - Evenness of Spirit 68
  - Serenity 69
  - Self Forgetfulness 70

6. CALVARY
  - Calvary is the Mount of Love 72
  - Mount Calvary is the True School of Love 73

PART II

ADDITIONAL SELECTIONS
FOR
HEALTH AND GROWTH
IN THE
SPIRITUAL LIFE

7. GOD'S ACTION UPON US
  - Spiritual Direction 79
  - Method for Meditation 80
  - Contemplation 82
  - Loving Recollection in Contemplation 84

8. OUR COOPERATION WITH GOD'S ACTION
  - Divine Gifts 89
  - Patience 91
  - Humility 93

8. OUR COOPERATION WITH GOD'S ACTION - Cont'd.
    - Gentleness 96
    - Obedience 98
    - Commentary on Obedience 99
    - Chastity 101
    - Poverty 102
    - Simplicity 104

9. COUNSELS
    - Temptations 109
    - Disquietude 111
    - Sadness 113
    - Spiritual Consolations 115
    - Spiritual Dryness 116
    - Desires 119
    - Will of God 120
    - Union of Our Will with God's Good Pleasure 122

10. ST. PAUL'S EXHORTATION
    - St. Paul's Wonderful Exhortation
        to an Ecstatic Life, Lived Above Nature 127

NOTES 129

PREFACE

An attentive reader of the writings of St. Francis de Sales will discover in the *Directory* the essence of Salesian spirituality:

- joyful love of God
- evenness of spirit
- obedience to the will of God
- the overcoming of egotism, rather than exterior asceticism
- interior prayer
- contemplation
- the following of the life of Jesus

This work presents in an abridged form a large part of the important writings of the Saint, as contained in the *Introduction to a Devout Life, The Love of God,* and the books of *Letters.*

If we want to remain faithful to the experience and wisdom of centuries, we will freely choose to follow this way. We find in it a guide and spiritual stance to be taken by the Christian who wishes to live not only for the here and now, but also for eternity.

Many details of the *Directory* are to be seen only as suggestions. When Francis speaks of liberty of spirit, he approves of freedom in the choice of thoughts and interior inspirations. His gentle spirit often suggests and urges, rather than commands. At the same time, however, his spirituality implies a total gift of self to God in love and surrender, which leads the faithful Christian to holiness. The genius and charism of Francis are total love of God and neighbor lived out in deep humility and great gentleness.

A WORD OF ADVICE

My dear Reader,

A word of advice may be helpful before you take up this book to read its message. You may feel the practice of the *Spiritual Directory* is too demanding, too difficult for you to attempt to follow. A total gift of self to God and neighbor is asked. However, St. Francis de Sales, who knew human nature so well, is most encouraging. He tells us, one learns to love God by simply loving Him. He also knew, in order to do this and to persevere in growing in love for Him, certain guidelines promise a safer and happier journey or flight. Think of an airplane. Before taking off to the skies the wheels are firmly on the ground. Very slowly the pilot sets it into motion, coasts along the runway, picks up momentum and then takes off to the heights. A similar process takes place while beginning the flight to holiness through the *Spiritual Directory*. Begin by taking small steps and practice one or two points of the *Directory,* such as the "Direction of Intention" and short prayers throughout the day. Keep the book near you and every day, read reflectively a little from the commentaries, which explain how to practice the points of the *Directory.* In this way the good habit will be formed to open yourself to God's love and to His gifts. When you feel ready, take up a new point and little by little integrate the *Directory* into your life.

You may experience some bitterness in the beginning, as St. Francis de Sales foresees, in trying to be faithful to your good resolutions. Very soon, however, our Saint predicts, this book will become sweet to your palate through the abundance of God's love in your life.

The Holy Spirit has spoken through Vatican II in our times, "Holiness is for everyone," reiterating the message of Jesus, "You must be made perfect as your heavenly Father is perfect." (Matt. 5:48) The Lord could not impose impossibilities on us. Rather, He is a faithful God who desires His children to become like Him.

ACKNOWLEDGMENTS

Divine Providence chose our dear friend, Father John Conmy, O.S.F.S., to bring about the initiation and work of *In the Midst of the World*. Father asked me to translate from German into English the *Spiritual Directory* of St. Francis de Sales, which the Oblates in Austria have published for people in the world. Under Father's invaluable direction and guidance, a much larger work developed, hopefully everything that is needed to lead the reader to holiness.

I will always be deeply grateful to Father Conmy for his complete interest, encouragement and prayer for the success of this work. My wholehearted and sincerest thanks go to Father for all he has meant in the writing of the book.

Sister Mary Aimee Franklin, V.H.M., has worked with me for countless hours in entire dedication and joy to update, edit and give a newer look to the writings of our beloved Saint. I will always cherish with loving gratitude all that Sister Aimee has done to give the book its present appearance.

Sister Alice Patricia Dolan, C.S.J., with whom I consulted a number of times, through very significant questions and insights, inspired the writing of "Origin of the Spiritual Directory" and "How to Practice IN THE MIDST OF THE WORLD." Sister, moreover, was instrumental in assisting me to realize that dividing the book into two parts will present a clearer way of understanding the *Spiritual Directory*. To Sister Alice Patricia, my sincerest gratitude for her warm interest and most helpful comments and suggestions.

xviii

Sister Judith Ann Shea, C.S.J., made me happy indeed when she readily accepted the invitation to create illustrations for various pages of the *Directory* to enhance the written message. I thank Sister for the beautiful and meaningful illustrations.

We owe our deepest gratitude to Mary and Phil Halsey for their untiring work and invaluable help in the printing of this book.

Tan Publications very kindly gave permission to use excerpts from the *Love of God,* by John K. Ryan, for *In the Midst of the World.*

ORIGIN OF THE
SPIRITUAL DIRECTORY

In 1610 St. Francis de Sales, a man not only of his own time, but also ahead of his time, felt inspired to write the *Introduction to a Devout Life* for the laity. Centuries before Vatican II, Francis believed holiness is for everyone. All are called to open themselves to God's love and so to become holy.

As a young student at the University of Padua, Francis wrote a way of life for himself, a *Spiritual Directory*. Having found these guidelines to holiness most helpful, he lived by them throughout his life. Later he also gave them to his Novices for the direction of their daily actions.

Francis asks the question, "How do you learn to love God?" and answers, "By loving Him. There is no other way." His approach to holiness is a simple one. Gently he shows how to set one foot before the other, in climbing the steep ladder of the love of God. Doing all our actions, both great and small, with a great love for God, prepares our heart to receive His love, to live always in His presence, to surrender and to become one with Him and His holy will, and so to reach intimate union. In this is found holiness.

In our own time, Vatican II, inspired by the Spirit of God, revealed clearly that holiness is for all of God's people, the laity as well as clergy. Today there is a great urgency, a hunger for God, for love, for security - as we experience tragedies resulting from crime, waning morality, and the breaking up of families. Such frustrating situations cause great pain and unhappiness in the hearts of so many. If individuals everywhere were brought to a deep realization of God's love for them, their lives would shine radiantly. They would witness to God's love in joy, in a society grown weary and disillusioned.

In His covenant promise to Abraham, God said, "Do not fear, I am your shield; I will make your reward very great." (Gen. 15:1) This same covenant love is ours today to strengthen us to take heart and to launch out confidently to accept this love. God Himself will be our reward, exceedingly great. Where does it begin? In your heart and mine!

May St. Francis de Sales, Doctor of the Church, encourage us to take up this simple spiritual guide, which led him to holiness in the midst of the world. It is a sure way to the love of God and neighbor, wholeness and ultimate happiness. Moreover, the *Spiritual Directory* portrays, spells out and presents the Gospel message in a livable way.

HOW TO PRACTICE THE SPIRITUAL DIRECTORY "IN THE MIDST OF THE WORLD"

In the Midst of the World combines the *Spiritual Directory* of St. Francis de Sales with selections from his other writings. The *Spiritual Directory* is a full expression of the Gospel message as lived, taught and promoted by Francis. These pages are designed to help everyone find inspiration and courage to live a love relationship with God and neighbor.

In Part I of the book, the *Spiritual Directory* itself is arranged on the pages on the left side. These contain what is to be put into practice and assimilated into one's life. On the pages opposite are found selections which add insight and understanding on how to practice each part - all taken from other writings of the Saint. Commentaries have been written for further explanation on the "Great Intention," "Direction of Intention," "Prayer," "The Measure of Love of Neighbor," and "Obedience."

In Part II, the additional selections are meant to promote health and growth in the spiritual life. The method for meditation, as presented in Chapter Two, becomes an important tool for progress in prayer for beginners. With time, mental prayer leads to contemplation, which is described in Chapters Three and Four.

The spiritual life is often beset by temptations, trials, dryness and similar sufferings. The Chapters treating with these difficulties contain encouraging and strengthening advice. St. Francis de Sales' exposition of how to discover and discern the will of God is like a beacon lighting up the way. Francis also gives a masterly description of the virtues to be practiced in a life lived according to the Gospel message. Suffering and the Cross find a prominent place in his writings, since he sees these as treasures which prove our love of God and gain us the prize, eternal glory.

Little by little, as we make these messages our own, and live them out, we will experience the meaning of the words of St. Paul, "You will be able to grasp fully the breadth and length and the height and depth of Christ's love, and experience this love, which surpasses all knowledge, so that you may attain to the fullness of God Himself." (Eph. 3:18-19)

May we take to heart the challenge of Vatican II to all people:

> It is evident to everyone that all the faithful of Christ, of whatever rank or status, are called to the fullness of the Christian life and to the perfection of charity. By this holiness a more human way of life is promoted, even in this earthly society. (DOCUMENTS OF VATICAN II, *Lumen Gentium, #40)*

This is an echo of St. Francis de Sales' basic inspiration, that all are called to holiness.

JACOB'S LADDER [1]

Jacob's Ladder is an excellent picture of the devout life, the life lived for God. The two uprights represent prayer, which obtains for us the love of God and the Sacraments which confer it. The rungs of the ladder are the steps of love. On these, one descends by action to help and support one's neighbor, or ascends by contemplation to loving union with God.

On the ladder are persons who have angelic hearts, who are full of vigor and devotion. They have wings to fly and soar up towards God by holy prayer, but they also have feet to walk with their neighbor in caring and mutual concern. Their faces are beautiful and cheerful because they receive all things with peace and joy. Their thoughts, affections and actions have no other motive than to please God. They make use of this world, but in a way which is altogether pure and sincere, since they take only what is necessary for their condition in life. Wherever we are we may and ought to aspire to the perfect life.

Devotion is the queen of divine gifts, because it is the perfection of charity. True and living devotion presupposes the love of God, or rather, it is nothing else but a true love of God.

Insofar as divine love beautifies our souls, makes us pleasing to God and gives us a share in His very life, it is called *grace*. Insofar as it gives us strength to do good, it is *charity*. When it reaches such a degree of perfection that we do good carefully, frequently and readily, it becomes *devotion*.

Since devotion consists in a certain excelling degree of charity, it prompts us to not only observe all the commandments of God, but also to do readily and heartily as many good works as we can, even though they are only counseled and inspired.

True devotion, however, must be practiced in different ways by the nobleman and by the working man, by the servant and the prince, by the widow, by the unmarried girl, and by the married woman. Moreover, the practice of devotion must be adapted to the strength, to the occupation and to the duties of each one in particular.

Tell me, is it proper for a bishop to want to lead a solitary life like a Carthusian; or for married people to be no more concerned than a Capuchin about increasing their income; or for a working man to spend his whole day in church like a religious? Is not this sort of devotion unorganized and intolerable? Yet, this error occurs frequently. However, in no way does true devotion destroy anything at all. On the contrary it perfects and fulfills all things and even enhances them. In fact, if it ever works against anyone's legitimate station and calling, then it is very definitely false.

Just as every gem cast in honey becomes brighter and more sparkling, so each person becomes more acceptable and fitting in his or her own vocation when they practice devotion. Through it your family cares become more peaceful, mutual love between husband and wife becomes more sincere, and our work, no matter what it is, becomes more pleasant and agreeable.

It is an error to wish to exclude devotion from our lives. There are types of devotion fit for perfecting those who live in a secular state. True and solid devotion embraces with a resolute, prompt and active will everything it knows to be pleasing to God.

PART I

THE SPIRITUAL DIRECTORY
AND
COMMENTARIES

Chapter 1

FAITHFULNESS IN ALL THINGS

Spiritual Directory

THE GREAT INTENTION

May your whole life and everything you do tend to unite you with God.

May your prayers, good works and the practice of the Christian virtues, above all that of charity, contribute to the life of the Church and to the salvation of your neighbor.

For this reason, may you desire nothing so much as to live an intensely spiritual life. Then, while pleasing God, your power for good will be communicated to the hearts of the faithful.

Selection from the Saint

HOW TO APPLY OUR WORKS MORE PARTICULARLY TO THE LOVE OF GOD [2]

To make true spiritual progress, it is necessary to direct our whole lives and all our actions to God. We do this by offering and consecrating to Him all we do every day in the morning exercise, as is taught in the *Introduction to a Devout Life* and found in Part I of this book. In this daily renewal of our commitment to God, we give glory to Him and spread the virtue of love over all our actions.

Let us also join our lives to God's love, by sending aspirations (short prayers) to Him hundreds of times during the day, centering our hearts on Him. This practice not only casts our spirit constantly into God, but also directs all our actions to Him. How does one, who at every moment desires to love, not also do all one's deeds in God and for God? Frequent aspirations will accomplish this, for example: "My God and my All!"; "Jesus, you are my life. Grant me the grace to die to myself, that I may live entirely for you."; "My Beloved is wholly mine, and I am wholly His." (Cant. 2:16); or any other aspirations you may choose. Happy is that person who, once for all, makes a perfect dedication of self into the hands of God.

Commentary on the "Great Intention"

At the outset as we begin our spiritual journey, or if we have already advanced on it, let us be convinced that St. Francis de Sales is a gentle, yet sure guide on the road to holiness.

In the first point of the *Spiritual Directory* he asks us to live an intensely spiritual life, so that while pleasing God, our power for good will be communicated to the hearts of the faithful.

Holiness, as our Saint presents it, is meant for everyone, not just for some elect few whom the Church canonizes. Francis took seriously our Lord's mandate, "You must be made perfect as your heavenly Father is perfect." (Matt. 5:48) How can we reach this holiness about which Jesus speaks? Francis focuses our attention on the *Spiritual Directory*. He describes these guidelines as a sweet and easy means to reach the perfection of charity, if we seriously try to discover all the treasures hidden in them.

In Baptism God's own life has been poured into us. The life of the Blessed Trinity, Father, Son and Holy Spirit, pulsates in our very hearts. "You are precious in my eyes and glorious, because I love you." (Is. 43:4) Therefore, God desires—with an infinite desire—that we love Him in return, that His life may deepen and grow in us, so that we may reach intimate union with Him, even here in this earthly life.

Just as our bodies need food constantly to grow and remain strong and healthy, so our spiritual life must be fed and nourished over and over, if we want to grow strong in the Spirit and become holy. St. Francis supplies this food, this nourishment in a simple, but very effective way. His method includes:

    1) frequent aspirations and short prayers throughout the day,

     2) the direction of our intention to the love of God
before each action,

     3) living in His presence in spiritual Retreats.

These practices are described in their respective Chapters.

    There is another dimension contained in this point
of the *Directory*. We are told, "If we live an intensely
spiritual life, while pleasing God, our power for good will
be communicated to the hearts of the faithful." *Lumen
Gentium #40* presents this concept in our own day by
stating clearly that, "All the faithful are called to the
fullness of the Christian life and the perfection of charity,
and by this holiness a more human way of life is promoted
even in this earthly society."

    We, the people of God, who make up the Body of
Christ, are closely related to each other. The joys and sufferings, the hunger and poverty, the loneliness and fears,
the needs of each member: these must become our concern
if we claim to love Christ intimately. How can we practice
this Christian love, this unselfish way of giving ourselves
away numberless times as we face the challenge and reality
of each new day?

    It is precisely the faithful practice of the *Directory*
which will impel us to be willing to die to self and to live for
God and for others. Our openness to the Father's gracious
will, our holy intentions offered in union with Jesus, which
will deepen His life within us and His love, this tremendous
power for good, burning in our hearts, will effect a more
human way of life. We shall become co-creators, co-
redeemers with Christ to help raise up a fallen society.

    A beautiful example of such a life of love and offering
in our own century is St. Therese of Lisieux. Her shining
example is worthy of imitation. It is of interest to note
that her older sister Pauline, who had been educated by
the Sisters of the Visitation in Le Mans, France, instructed
Therese as a young girl in this spirituality through which
she reached holiness in a short time.

Spiritual Directory

DIRECTION OF INTENTION

Persons who desire to grow and make progress in the following of Christ must, at the beginning of all their actions, ask grace.

Let them stand firm in the present moment to perceive GOD'S BIDDING

- "HIS HOLY INTENTION" -

and offer to Him all the good they may do.

Even in the face of obstacles, let them carry out God's will quietly and perseveringly to the end, receiving all from His Fatherly hand. He will afterwards reward them out of the abundance of His love.

In the mind of the Apostle Paul, all we do should be done in the name of God, and to please Him. (1 Cor.10:13) (Col.3:17)

Nothing is too insignificant or ordinary that we cannot discover in it the will of God. The preparation of meals, recreation and even life-restoring rest belong to this category.

Selection from the Saint

THE VALUE OF SMALL ACTIONS[3]

Great opportunities to serve God are rare; little ones are always present. But he who is faithful in little things will be placed over great things. (Matt. 25:21)

Opportunities are offered hourly for us to perform with great love seemingly unimportant works. Gentleness and patience toward others, overcoming our own moods and inclinations, acknowledging within ourselves our own imperfections, and persevering effort to keep ourselves tranquil and at peace: this faithfulness is of greater value than we can imagine.

"To do little actions with great purity of intention and a strong will to please God is to do them excellently, and then they greatly sanctify us." The more our works are motivated by the love of God, the greater their value becomes.

Some persons weigh the merit of their actions by their appearance or difficulty. They prize only showy virtues or gifts, without considering that the use they make of God's gifts derives value only from the motive and aim of their actions. Charity must be the only measure.

Commentary on the "Direction of Intention"

In this point of the *Directory* we will discover how to make rapid progress on our spiritual journey, if we but explore the tremendous possibilities for love and holiness hidden therein.

At the beginning of all our actions, whether great or small, important or unimportant, we are to ask grace of our Lord to perform that action for love of Him and then offer to Him all the good we may do. A short aspiration, such as "All for love of You, Oh Jesus, grant me Your boundless love and grace," will express this desire.

No matter what our vocation in life may be— whether wife and mother, taking care of the children and performing household duties, or husband and father, earning a living for the family, whether teacher or student, factory worker or bank president, Priest or Religious—by being faithful and asking God's grace, and by offering our actions to Him out of love throughout the day, we will make tremendous strides on the road to holiness. New vistas will open to the eyes of our souls, where we will begin to see God and His great goodness in everyone and in everything. Through the purity of our intentions, we truly will be living in the spirit of that beautiful beatitude: "Blessed are the pure of heart, for they shall see God." (Matt. 5:8)

We can at the same time include the needs of others in our love offerings, so that God's kingdom may come and His love may reign in the hearts of all who are dear to us, and of countless others. We are not just content with becoming holy ourselves, but we would desire that the good God be loved in the hearts of all.

The *Directory* continues by asking us to stand firm in the present moment. How deep and touching is this mystery of love in the present moment on the part of God in regard to our individual lives!

Reflect in the following way: *the great God is intent on me, offering a love gift to me in the duty of this present moment, planned or permitted uniquely for me from all eternity. No one else in the world could take my place to give to God this particular gift. I feel impelled to respond to "God's bidding, His holy intention" by accepting His gift and offering it back to Him in love. This total openness to God will constantly deepen my relationship with Him and bring about that union which He so desires. From this oneness with the Lord will flow that peace and joy which ought to mark the life of every Christian. Moreover, my life will become an unmistakable witness to His presence in the world.*

There is one more very important aspect of faith contained in this "Direction of Intention," that is, suffering.

We are told, "Even in the face of obstacles, let them carry out God's will quietly and perseveringly to the end, receiving all from His Fatherly hand. He will afterwards reward them with the abundance of His love." St. Francis is a genius in directing our gaze upward beyond the immediate obstacle, which could include any suffering, such as illness, misunderstandings, inclement weather, failure in an undertaking, or the many unexpected, difficult situations which we experience during any given day.

We are, first of all, to receive them from the Fatherly hand of God. What a difference this image of the strong, supporting hand of the Father will make in our attitude and acceptance. "I have carved you in the palm of my hand," (Is. 49:16) is an expression of love and care and concern. If we carried this image in our hearts and made it our own to cling to in times of stress, we would experience God's personal love in our lives. In fact any suffering which our Father sends or permits is a desire on His part to help us to grow in love and trust and to surrender to His will, so that He may afterwards reward us with the abundance of His love. What deep insight our Saint manifests into the great mystery of suffering! If we but accept these precious occasions of trials and difficulties patiently from the Fatherly hand of God and carry out His will quietly and perseveringly to the end, He will reward us not only with His love, but with an abundance of His love.

From experience we know that every day brings with it many opportunities where we can learn to accept these treasures patiently and humbly. In return our Father is waiting to reward us with an out-pouring of His tender love.

In conclusion, nothing is insignificant in the eyes of the Father, if offered to Him in love. This includes those everyday actions we enjoy, such as eating, drinking, and recreating, as well as resting in order to restore our energies.

Chapter 2

PRAYER

Spiritual Directory

PRAYER

Begin each prayer, the silent as well as the vocal, by being aware of the presence of God. Keep to this without exception.

In all petitions and prayers, the ''we'' carries weight, as the Lord taught us in the *Our Father*. In it, no ''I'' or ''for me'' is found.

Before all else, the prayer of the mind and heart is recommended to you, most especially that which has as its object the life and Passion of the Lord.

By frequent contemplation you will be grasped by Him, and you will learn to carry out all your actions as He did.

Selection from the Saint

THE NECESSITY OF PRAYER[4]

Prayer is most necessary to help us to understand divine things and to open our wills to the warmth of heavenly love. It cleanses our souls of their imperfections and lessens our passions.

By frequent meditation on the life and Passion of our Lord, your whole soul will be filled with Him. You will learn His dispositions, and you will model your actions after His. He is the light of the world by Whom we must be illuminated. He is the living well of Jacob, cleansing and renewing us. In our prayers it is most appropriate and profitable for us to consider and contemplate His life, death and resurrection.

Contemplative prayer is not an aimless roving of the mind. It is not difficult to send short, intimate thoughts to God, weaving them often into all work and occupations. Speak those words with the heart or with the mouth which love inspires at the moment. One who is filled with human love has his thoughts almost always with the object of his love. If the loved one is absent, he does not miss an opportunity to express his feelings in letters. Similarly, those who love God think of Him, breathe for Him, strive for Him, speak of Him. Everything serves as inspiration to this and effects a lifting up of the mind to God.

Spiritual Directory

MEDITATION

Let us learn, as is suggested further on in Part II, to meditate after the instructions of St. Francis de Sales, as he describes in the *Introduction to a Devout Life* and the *Treatise on the Love of God.*

An important element of meditation is the preparation of the day. This means reflecting on the different events which may possibly occur during the day. This will dispose you to act well and to make right decisions at the proper moment.

If for some reason you are unable to make this mental prayer in the morning, try to make it at some other time during the day.

Selection from the Saint

PREPARATION FOR MEDITATION[5]

Perhaps you do not know how to make mental prayer. I will give you a simple and brief method to begin to practice it. In the beginning, four thoughts can be beneficial in helping us to become aware of the presence of God. We may consider:

(1) *The omnipresence of God.* Just as the birds, wherever they fly, encounter the air, so we find God wherever we are. We do not see God, although Faith tells us of His presence. If we do not think about Him at all, it is just as if we knew it not. Therefore, before prayer we must always stir ourselves up to an attentive consideration of His presence.

(2) *His presence in the ground of our being.* God is within us in a special manner. As St. Paul says: "In God we live and move and have our being." Considering this truth, you will stir up in your heart a great reverence for God, Who is so intimately present there. He is there as the heart of your heart, and the spirit of your spirit.

(3) *Our Savior in Heaven.* Though we do not perceive Him, He looks at us with great love. From heaven He beholds all people in the world, His children, and more particularly those who are in prayer.

(4) *Our Savior in His Sacred Humanity.* Think of the Savior as though He were near you, just as you would represent your friends to yourself. If, however, you are before the Blessed Sacrament of the Altar, this presence of Jesus is real and not only in the imagination.

Commentary on "Prayer"

To find God, to experience His presence in our lives, and to make progress on our way to holiness, it is very important that we go apart some time every day to pray. The atmosphere of a quiet room, the Eucharistic presence in a church, or perhaps at times a beautiful outdoor nature scene can be conducive to deep prayer. It is also very possible to find the Lord waiting for us in our hearts in a crowded bus or subway train, if no other time or space is available. The suggested method, as St. Francis de Sales presents it, is an excellent one.

The morning hours lend themselves especially well to prayer. Then again toward evening, after the day's work, our souls need to be renewed and refreshed in moments of mental or centering prayer. We will receive inspiration, courage and strength to continue to imitate our Lord and to practice the Christian virtues. The quality of our prayer determines the quality of our lives.

St. Francis de Sales directed many persons in their life of prayer. His insights are invaluable. At one time he shared an experience of his own in a letter to St. Jane de Chantal.

> For the last three days it has been an exquisite pleasure to reflect on the great honor the heart has in speaking alone to its God alone. Is not this a marvelous secret? The Doctors of the Church say, to pray, it is well to think that there is no one in the world but God. This thought can deeply and strongly influence the soul and cause the application to be made with incomparably greater force. (Letter CDVIII)

It is in prayer that God will reveal His unique and intimate love for us, that love which desires to be diffused and poured out into our hearts as if we were the only one in the world.

In another place our Saint wrote to St. Jane:

> It is a good prayer and a good way of keeping oneself in the presence of God to hold fast to the will of God and to His good pleasure. (Letter DCCCXXXVIII)

And again:

> Go to prayer with great meekness of spirit, without wanting to do anything there except to receive from our Lord what He will give you. Let it be enough for you to be in His presence although you neither see nor feel Him and though you cannot represent Him to yourself. Begin by an act of faith and from time to time look if you cannot get sight of Him. (Letter MMLXXXII)

This sound advice may be most helpful during times of dryness or difficulty in prayer.

Still at another time he told her:

> Your prayer of simply committing yourself to God is extremely holy and salutary. Never doubt this.
>
> (Letter MLX)

Attempting to rid ourselves of distractions is the lot of all of us. St. Francis suggests a simple remedy:

> When your heart wanders bring it back quietly to its subject and tenderly place it close to its Master. If you do nothing else the whole time of prayer than bring your heart back and place it again beside our Lord, although each time you do so it turns away from Him, your hour will be very well spent and you will be giving a great deal of pleasure to our Lord. (Letter MCCCXXV)

How consoling these words are for those who may be discouraged at times about their distractions during prayer.

To one woman St. Francis gave this advice:

> The best prayer or state of prayer is that which keeps us so well occupied with God that we have no thought of ourselves or of what we are doing. In a word, we must go

to prayer in good earnest, simply, artlessly, to be with God, lovingly uniting ourselves to Him. True love hardly needs a method. (Letter MCDXLI)

In another place St. Francis continues:

Do not be distressed if sometimes, or even very often, you are not consoled by your meditations. Persevere gently, humbly, patiently, without forcing your mind. Read a book when fatigued; read a little, then meditate, then read a little again, and again meditate until the end of your half hour. I have tried this and found it helpful. The grace of meditation cannot be gained by any effort of the mind, but by a meek and loving perseverance abounding in humility. (Letter CCXLI)

Let us have confidence that, if we carefully follow these inspired suggestions, the Lord Himself will lead us to holiness.

Commentary on *"Prayer of Praise"*

PRAYER OF PRAISE

Holiness, in the spirit of St. Francis de Sales, means happiness.

As Christians, we are exhorted by St. Paul to rejoice always. "Rejoice always in the Lord, again I say rejoice!" (Phil. 4:4) To attain to this happy state of mind and heart we must be sure to praise the Lord continuously in our hearts. God's infinite power and strength, His eternal wisdom and love are all ours for the asking.

• Before beginning any particular task, we can praise the Lord with a simple prayer, such as: "Jesus, I praise and thank You for taking care of what I am about to do. Your infinite power, wisdom, goodness and strength are all mine. •I surrender to You, lean upon You, depend on You. I trust You with all my heart." Do this particularly when some difficulty comes upon you, since anything which disturbs or robs you of your peace of mind and joy of heart is not from God. Then continue your simple prayer of praise, concentrating on the goodness, power, wisdom and strength of the Lord.

Jesus Himself praised the Father in this way. Before raising Lazarus to life He said to Martha: "Did I not assure you that if you believed you would see the glory of God displayed?" Then he continued: "Father, I thank You for having heard me. I know that You always hear me." (John 11:40-42) We will also see the glory of God revealed to us by attuning our hearts and minds to this positive attitude, through which we will not only overcome all thoughts of fear, worry, cowardice, jealousy, anger, attachments, and uncharity; but our whole person will be filled with the divine healing, joy, strength and vigor of Jesus Who lives within us, and Who has said: "All this I tell you that my joy may be yours and that your joy may be complete." (John 15:11)

Practicing this prayer of praise is stepping out in faith and taking Jesus at His word: "I have come that they may have life and have it to the full." (John 10:10)

Then, indeed, will the words of St. Francis de Sales in his *Spiritual Directory* come true for us: "If we accept everything from the loving hand of the Father, He will afterwards reward us with the abundance of His love."

Commentary on "Contemplation"

CONTEMPLATION AND HOW TO PREPARE FOR IT

In his book *The Love of God* St. Francis de Sales describes contemplation as being simply the mind's loving, unmixed, permanent attention to the things of God. Our Saint's *Spiritual Directory,* inspired by the Holy Spirit, is uniquely designed to prepare and lead those who practice it to a loving, unmixed, permanent attention to the things of God, namely, contemplation, union with God.

Many today ask: *how can I receive the gift of contemplation? What must I do? Where do I begin?* I believe we can affirm that the directives of the *Spiritual Directory,* namely, "The Great Intention," "The Direction of Intention," "Prayer," "Spiritual Retreat," and "Short Prayers Throughout the Day," lead those who are faithful to this way, to contemplation.

In Baptism God's own life has been poured into us. Father, Son and Holy Spirit favor us with their constant presence. This initial gift is brought to its full potential through our constant response in love. As to the Samaritan woman at Jacob's well, Jesus also speaks to us:

> If you only recognized God's gift and Who it is Who is asking you for a drink, you would have asked Him instead and He would have given you living water, which springs up to provide eternal life. (John 4:10, 14)

Yes, if only we knew and appreciated this free gift, this living water of grace which Jesus thirsts to give to us, we would never tire of asking for it. In the "Direction of Intention" of the *Spiritual Directory,* we possess a great tool to attain to this desirable goal. Since we are instructed to ask for grace before each of our various actions, occupations and prayers, and to offer these lovingly to God, He in turn will fill us more and more with His own life, the living water of our souls.   As we continue on our spiritual journey, our faith, trust and love deepen.   His gracious presence will permeate all events and circumstances of our lives.   We will see and recognize His love and action in everyone and in everything.   Our lives will be truly contemplative as described by St. Francis de Sales: "Contemplation is simply the mind's loving, unmixed, permanent attention to the things of God."

Our destiny, the very reason for our creation, is to know and love and contemplate God and all His creation for all eternity.   This heavenly life, however, must and does begin here and now.   We will find it if we but open our hearts to it.   Every moment of time touches eternity. The eternal value of each passing moment is determined by the quality of our love of God and neighbor.   St. Francis de Sales places within easy reach a way to perform our actions with great love of God and so, attain to holiness, a life of contemplation, the summit of charity.

Chapter 3

PRAYER OF THE HEART
THROUGHOUT THE DAY

Spiritual Directory

PRAYER OF THE HEART THROUGHOUT THE DAY

There are five kinds of shorter prayers which flow out of our daily mental prayer. They are described in the following pages and include:

I. **PREPARATION FOR THE DAY** — **Morning Exercise**

    A. *Think.* Thank God and adore Him for preserving you during the night. Ask His forgiveness for any faults or sins you may have committed.

    B. *Consider.* The gift of the present day is a preparation for eternity. Make a firm resolution to use the day well for this intention.

    C. *Look Ahead.* Foresee opportunities in which to serve God. Anticipate whatever temptations might occur. Prepare yourself by a good resolution to avoid carefully whatever might be against God's glory and your salvation. Then, consider how you plan to carry out this resolution.

    D. *Humble Yourself.* Acknowledge your dependence upon God. Hold your heart in your hands and offer it to His love, together with your good intentions. Ask His protection, His strength, that you be successful in His service.

Be brief and fervent in this prayer and never omit it before leaving your room. Then God's blessing will be upon all that you do throughout the day.

Selections from the Saint

HOW WE SHOULD RECEIVE INSPIRATIONS[6]

By inspirations we mean all the interior attractions, movements, reproaches, all the lights and rays of knowledge, which God causes within us through His Fatherly love and care. By giving these blessings, He desires to awaken us, to urge and attract us to the practice of virtues, to love, and to good resolutions.

The pleasure we take in inspirations is a great step to the glory of God. We already begin to please Him by it. It is the consent which perfects the virtuous act. If after receiving the inspiration and taking pleasure in it, we refuse to give our consent to God, we greatly displease Him.

RECOMMENDATION TO GOD
(Practiced by St. Francis)

"I recommend myself to You, O my God. I place myself entirely, with all that belongs to me, into the hands of Your eternal Goodness. I beg You to look upon me as being completely given up to You. I leave You absolutely the care of my person, what I am and what You wish me to be. To You do I recommend my soul, my mind, my heart, my memory, my understanding, my will. Grant me the grace that with all these faculties of my being I may serve You, love You, please You and adore You forever."

Spiritual Directory

II. QUIET INTERVAL WITH THE LORD

Before the evening meal, take time to recollect yourself in some quiet place, or before the Blessed Sacrament. Place yourself in the presence of Jesus Crucified by an interior glance and simple consideration. Rekindle the fire of love in your heart. Humble yourself. Make loving aspirations toward your Divine Savior.

If you wish, you may reflect on an appropriate passage from Scripture.

III. NIGHT PRAYER — Examination of Conscience

Before retiring, thank God for all the blessings of the day. Glance briefly over your thoughts, words, moods, feelings and actions. If you discover a fault, examine your motivation, ask God's pardon and resolve to amend. Always be faithful to this practice!

Recommend to God's care your soul and body, the Church, your relatives and friends. Ask the Blessed Virgin, your Guardian Angel and the Saints to watch over you. Then, with God's blessing upon you, seek the rest which He desires for you.

Selection from the Saint

HOW WE SHOULD CARRY OUT INSPIRATIONS[7]

Resolve to accept with a good heart all the inspirations God gives to you. Consider the love which inspired them. Consent to them lovingly and steadfastly. In important or extraordinary matters, that you may not be deceived, always ask counsel of your Director and obey him with humility.

In carrying out inspirations, put them into effect with great care, for this is the height of true virtue. Practicing well the prayer of the heart and the morning exercise is of wonderful help towards all this. In this way, we prepare ourselves to do what is good, not only in a general manner, but also in particular situations.

Spiritual Directory

IV. ATMOSPHERE OF SPIRITUAL RETREAT

It is here that I wish you very earnestly to follow my counsel, for in this exercise of spiritual retreat — short prayers, Scripture phrases, speaking to Christ throughout the day — lies one of the surest means of your spiritual advancement and the great work of devotion. Without it the contemplative life cannot be properly followed, nor the active life lived well. It can supply the lack of all other prayers, but the failure of it can scarcely be made good in any other way. I beg you, therefore, to embrace it with your whole heart and never abandon it.

Selection from the Saint

LIVING IN GOD'S PRESENCE[8]

Recall the presence of God as often as you can during the day by one of the four ways I pointed out to you. You will see God's eyes fixed upon you with incomparable love. You will say: "Why do You think of me so often, Lord, and why do I think of You so seldom?"

Allow your heart to retire frequently every day to some place, either on Mount Calvary or in the wounds of our Lord, or in some other place near Him. You will be refreshed and recreated there, in the midst of exterior occupations, or even while engaged in discussions or transactions with others, as in a stronghold, and you will find it a defense against temptation. Then you can truly say to our Lord, "You are my house of refuge, my security."

This mental solitude cannot be hindered by those around you. Your heart remains alone in the presence of God.

Seldom are our tasks so important as to keep us from withdrawing our hearts from them from time to time in order to retire into this divine solitude.

Separated from all, you will say with David, "I have watched and become like a pelican in the wilderness. I have become like an owl in a ruined house and like a solitary sparrow on the housetop." These words show you in a mystical sense three excellent retreats, three hermitages, in which you can practice solitude in imitation of our Savior:

(1) On Mount Calvary He was like a pelican in the wilderness, who gives new life to her dying young ones with her own blood.

Reflect on the touching scene of the mother pelican who pierces her side to feed with her own blood the little dying pelicans gathered around her, to restore them to new life. Similarly, our Lord desired that His heart should be thrust through by a lance, that the Precious Blood flowing from this wound might cleanse you from all sin and impart to you His own divine life.

(2) At His birth in a deserted stable, He was like an owl in a ruined house, weeping over faults and sins.

Consider what love impelled Him to become a little infant to win your love. Try to impress deeply on your heart that this same little Child is the Eternal Word, ". . . the Word Who was in the beginning with God, Who became flesh and made His dwelling among us. Of His fullness we have all had a share — love following upon love." (John 1:1, 14, 16) In return, can you refuse Him any of the love of your heart?

(3) On the day of His Ascension, our Lord resembled the sparrow, ascending up to heaven.

Reflect upon and unite yourself to the great love with which He constantly intercedes for you to the Father for all your needs and those of the whole world.

In all three places you can make your retreat in the midst of pressing, exterior occupations; or you may choose any other place to which you are attracted.

Spiritual Directory

V. ASPIRATIONS AND EJACULATORY PRAYERS- SHORT PRAYERS AND SCRIPTURE PHRASES

Aspirations to God proceed from and are born of good thoughts.

Aspire then very often to God, by short but ardent movements of the heart.

Admire His beauty, invoke His help.

Place yourself in spirit at the foot of the Cross.

Adore His goodness, speak to Him frequently about your salvation.

Give Him your heart a thousand times a day.

Fix your interior eyes upon His sweetness.

Give Him your hand, as a little child does to his Father, that He may lead you.

Turn toward Him with an intense and tender love.

Holy, Holy, Holy

Holy LORD of love - praise to You

Jesus

Praise to You

Alleluia

Praise to You LORD

Thanks LORD

My LORD and My God

Jesus mercy

Selection from the Saint

THE USE OF ASPIRATIONS[9] -
SHORT PRAYERS AND SCRIPTURE PHRASES

There are certain aspirations, a way of speaking to God, which have special power to satisfy the heart. The Psalms of David are sewn with them. There are expressions of love found in the Canticle of Canticles and various invocations of the name of Jesus. For those who love God, every creature announces His praise. As St. Augustine says, everything in the world speaks to them of Him, in mute but intelligible language. St. Francis of Assisi, seeing a sheep all alone in the midst of a flock of goats, said to his companion, "See how gentle this poor little sheep is among the goats. So was Our Lord meek and humble among the Pharisees." At another time, seeing a little lamb devoured by a hog, he exclaimed, "Little lamb, how vividly you represent the death of my Savior!" Another, seeing a little chick beneath its mother's wing, said, "O Lord, protect me under the shadow of your wings." One may draw good thoughts and holy aspirations from whatever presents itself in life. Blessed are they who turn creatures to the glory of their Creator.

A soul, giving itself to interior and familiar conversation with God, will become beautiful with His perfections. This prayer of the heart can be interwoven easily with all our affairs and duties. The pilgrim who takes a little wine to rejoice his heart, though he stops for a short time, does not break off his journey, but gains strength to finish it more quickly and easily.

Chapter 4

SACRAMENTS
AND
THE WORD OF GOD

Spiritual Directory

SACRAMENT OF RECONCILIATION

Receive the Sacrament of Penance or Reconciliation humbly and devoutly, to be cleansed of all your sins. By confessing you are not only absolved from your sins, but also receive great strength to avoid them, a clear light to discern them well and abundant grace to repair all the loss they have caused you.

Have always a true sorrow for your sins, however small they may be, with a firm resolution to amend, for it is an abuse to confess any kind of sin without wishing to be cleansed of it. Many who confess out of custom or routine, without determination to correct themselves, remain burdened all their lives. This is a great spiritual loss.

Clear accusation should also include the motives and inclinations which led you to sin. The disclosure of the roots of the evil will enable your spiritual Father to know your heart better, to discern more clearly what remedies to suggest. Approach Confession with many other benefits in mind, realizing that contact with our Lord in this Sacrament has a deep healing effect on your life. In this one act of Confession, you will practice humility, obedience, simplicity, and more virtues than in any other action whatsoever.

Do not change your Confessor lightly, but continue to render him an account of your conscience, and consult with him about your advancement and growth. This type of spiritual direction, together with appropriate readings from Scripture, becomes a great means of progress in your life.

Selection from the Saint

RECONCILIATION [10]

Confession is something great, because in it we recognize the kindness of our Redeemer, Who shows us much mercy at all times.

Our faults should not discourage us, but be a reminder that in our weakness, God's power will be manifest more strongly. God's grace will support us. We look for this grace in the Sacrament of Penance and in the daily preparation for it, the examination of conscience.

Spiritual Directory

EUCHARISTIC MYSTERY

In order to offer the Eucharistic Sacrifice with the Priest to God the Father, for ourselves and the whole Church, we should strive to attend Mass daily. It is a great happiness for us human beings to participate through our prayer in such a sublime mystery. If it is impossible to attend the Eucharistic celebration in person, then at least let us join in it with our heart and spirit. Let us unite our thoughts with those of all Christians, as if we really assisted at Holy Mass.

COMMUNION

To unite yourself in love with our Lord in Holy Communion ought to be your greatest desire. Words and images from Holy Scripture may help to this end.

Our principal intention in Communion should be to advance, strengthen and console ourselves in the love of God, since we ought to receive for love's sake that which love alone gives us. The Savior cannot be considered in any action more loving or more tender than here, where He reduces Himself to the form of food to enter our souls. In this sacred meal, love prompts Him to unite Himself intimately with our hearts and bodies, so that we in turn may give ourselves in love and service to our neighbor.

After having received your Savior, give Him as warm a welcome as you can. Treat with Him of the affairs of your soul, behold Him within you, where He is present for your happiness. Conduct yourself in such a way that it may be known by all your actions that God is abiding in your heart.

Selection from the Saint

GREATNESS OF THE EUCHARISTIC MYSTERY[11]

The Eucharistic Sacrifice is the Sun of the spiritual exercises, the center of the Christian religion, the heart of devotion. This great mystery comprises within itself the abyss of divine charity. In it God gives Himself to us in total self-gift and communicates to us munificently His graces and favors.

When prayer is united with this divine Sacrifice it has an unspeakable force, so that the soul abounds with heavenly favors and flows with sweet delights. The Eucharistic Sacrifice stimulates us to love our neighbor heartily, since our Lord shed the last drops of His blood upon earth to make, as it were, a sacred mortar with which He would cement the faithful to one another, that there would never be any division among them.

The choirs of the Church in Glory, and those of the Church on earth, meet together and are united with our Lord in this divine action, so that with Him, in Him and through Him, they may ravish the heart of God the Father, and make His mercy all our own. What happiness for a soul to devoutly bring her affections as a contribution toward so precious and desirable a good!

By adoring and feeding on beauty, goodness and purity itself in this divine sacrament, you will become wholly beautiful, wholly good and wholly pure.

Spiritual Directory

THE WORD OF GOD AND SPIRITUAL READING

Be attentive to the Word of God, in whatever form it comes to you. Hear it always in openness and reverence, remembering that Jesus is present in His Word.

Read a little every day from Scripture and from a good book treating of the spiritual life or the lives of the Saints.

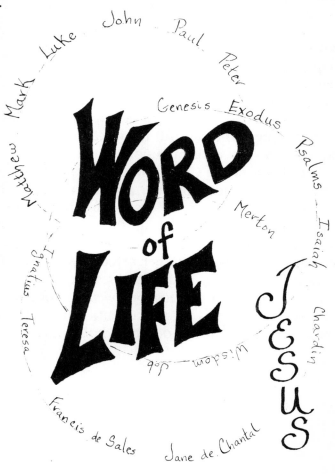

Selection from the Saint

IMPORTANCE OF THE WORD OF GOD AND SPIRITUAL READING[12]

Whether you listen to the Word of God in familiar conversation with your spiritual friends or in a homily, try to derive profit from it. Do not allow it to fall to the ground, but receive it into your heart. Imitate Our Lady who "carefully kept all these things in her heart."

Good spiritual books, including Scripture and the lives of the Saints, will reflect as in a mirror the Christian life. Look upon these as a message sent from heaven, to show you the way there and to give you the courage to walk along it.

Chapter 5

LIFE IN THE PRESENCE OF GOD

THE SEA SWALLOWS

Something remarkable is reported about the sea swallows. These small birds hatch at the seashore. They build nests so round and so tight that the sea water is not able to penetrate. At the top of each nest is a tiny opening through which the birds can fly in and out. The eggs are laid inside, permitting the young birds to live safely in the dry nests when the ocean overtakes them during a storm. The air contained in the nest serves as counterweight, so that it cannot tip over.

How much I desire that our hearts were the same, so completely firm, closed against the rebounding storms and the unrest of the world, that they stand open toward Heaven, to be present entirely for our Lord and for our neighbor.

Selection from the Saint

CARE AND DILIGENCE IN MANAGING OUR AFFAIRS [13]

The care and diligence we should have in managing our affairs are very different from solicitude, anxiety and eagerness. Care and diligence belong to charity, but anxiety and eagerness are contrary to happiness. God, having entrusted to you the affairs of your life, wills you to have great care of them. But try not to be excessively anxious or eager. Every kind of over-anxiety disturbs the reason and judgment, and hinders you, therefore, from doing well the very thing about which you are so eager.

Our Lord rebuked Martha because she was anxious and troubled about many things. If she had simply been careful, she would not have been troubled. Never was work carried out well which was done with impetuosity. We must make haste leisurely, as the proverb says. We always do a thing quickly enough when we do it well.

Receive then, in peace, the duties of your state in life and your appointed tasks, and try to carry them out in an orderly manner, so that you may not be weighed down or crushed under their burden. Above all, in whatever you do, rely wholly on the providence of God, since all your plans owe their success to that same providence. Cooperate with it by working tranquilly. Believe that if you put your trust in God, the results will always be the most profitable to you, though it may not always seem this way in your judgment.

While you are handling and gathering the goods of this world with one hand, always cling fast with the other to the hand of your heavenly Father. Turn to Him to see if what you are doing is pleasing to Him. Be careful not to let go of His hand or His protection, thinking to amass or gather more, for if He abondons you, you will not take a single step without falling on your face! When you are occupied with ordinary duties, look more on God than on what you are doing. If, however, important affairs demand your full concentration, turn to God from time to time. In this way, He will work with you, in you and for you, and your work will be followed by consolation.

"*If only God would seal my
heart, so that nothing
could ever enter there
but His divine Love,
and that nothing could open it
but charity!*"

St. Francis de Sales

Spiritual Directory

OCCUPATIONS AND STATE IN LIFE

When you are physically or mentally occupied,

while fulfilling the duties of your state in life,

renew as far as possible, again and again,

your "Yes" to the will of God.

Cast frequent interior glances

on the divine goodness.

This recalling of the presence of God

must be done gently and simply

without compulsion.

Selection from the Saint

FAITHFULNESS IN ALL THINGS[14]

Devout persons must take great care to serve God well in great and lofty things, as well as in little and lowly duties. We can equally touch the heart of God by our love, both by the one and by the other.

Be ready then to suffer many great afflictions for our Lord. Resolve to give Him all that is most precious to you, should it please Him to take it — father, mother, brother, sister, husband, wife, children, even your own life. You ought to prepare your heart to endure all such things. But as long as Providence does not send you great afflictions, at least bear patiently the little injuries, the small inconveniences, the trifling losses which you meet every day, for through these little occasions made use of with love, you will entirely win the heart of God and make it wholly yours.

These daily acts of charity, this headache, this ill-humor of a neighbor, this breaking of a glass, this small inconvenience of going to bed in time to rise early to pray and to participate in the Eucharist: all these little sufferings, when accepted and embraced with love, are extremely pleasing to the goodness of God. He promised a sea of perfect happiness for a cup of cold water given in His name. (Matt. 10:42) These opportunities which happen at every moment will deepen God's life within you.

St. Catherine of Sienna, Doctor of the Church, although favored with ecstasies, cooked meals in the convent kitchen and performed the lowliest household duties, seeing in them the will of God. It is important to direct rightly all our actions, however lowly they may be, to God's service.

Put your hands to strong things through prayer, receiving the Sacraments, giving the love of God to souls, infusing good inspirations into hearts — doing great and important works — according to your opportunities. But do not forget to practice little and humble virtues which, like flowers, grow at the foot of the Cross: the service of the poor, the care of the family and the diligence which never allows you to be idle. Perform these actions lovingly in the presence of God, to please Him and to become more like Him.

"*The loving Savior of our souls measures and adjusts all the events of this world to the advantage of those who - without reserve - give themselves to His divine Love.*"

St. Francis de Sales
(Letter CCCXIII)

Spiritual Directory

TO BECOME ALL THINGS TO ALL

Whether we are at work or leisure, the aspect of love of neighbor must always be present. This attitude toward the other, the ability to fit spontaneously into reality, has a decisive bearing on our selflessness and inner freedom.

To spread happiness, even when we are in low spirits, is considered not a small degree of virtue. Therefore, we must not join a community gathering thoughtlessly, but go with a clear attitude and a sense of religious responsibility.

the angel left her
There upon Mary set out
proceeding in haste
into the hill country
to a town in Judah
where she entered Zechariah's house
and greeted Elizabeth

Selection from the Saint

THE MEASURE OF LOVE OF NEIGHBOR[15]

We must remember that love has its seat in the heart. We can never love our neighbor too much, nor exceed the limits of reason in this affection, provided it dwells in the heart. St. Bernard said, "The measure of loving God is to love Him without measure," and that in our love there ought to be no limits. We should allow its branches to spread out as far as they possibly can. That which is said of love for God may also be understood to apply to our neighbor, provided the love of God always keeps the upper hand and holds the first rank.

We must not be content with loving our neighbor as ourselves, but we must take to heart our Lord's new commandment, "Love one another as I have loved you." (John 15:12) This means to love our neighbor more than ourselves. Our Lord always prefers us to Himself, and still does so every time we receive Him in Holy Communion, where He becomes our food. In a similar manner, He desires us to have such a love for one another that we shall always prefer our neighbor to ourselves. Our love ought to be so firm, cordial and solid that we should never refuse to do or suffer anything for our neighbor.

We must not be disappointed if we are not all equally gentle and sweet, provided that we love our neighbor with the love of our heart and to its fullest extent. To allow ourselves to be employed in things others will and we do not — which we do not choose — in this lies the highest point of abnegation. It is always incomparably better to do what others make us do (in that, of course, which is not contrary to God) than what we do and choose ourselves.

Let us then be steeped in gentleness towards our
neighbor, for we shall look upon everyone as resting in the
Heart of the Savior. Beholding him in that divine resting-
place, who would not love him, bear with him and be patient
with his imperfections? Your neighbor is there in the
Heart of the Savior, so beloved and so lovable, that the
divine Lover dies of love for him. Then the natural love of
relationship, good manners, sympathy and kindliness will
be purified and changed into the pure love of the divine
good pleasure. Those who aspire to perfection should
desire to be loved only with the love of charity, as our
Lord desires.[16]

Commentary on "Measure of Love of Neighbor"

St. Francis de Sales holds out to us, indeed, a high ideal of love of neighbor. The measure of loving him is comparable to that of loving God. There must be no limit to preferring our neighbor to ourselves in selfless love and giving. Jesus Himself gave us the example in word and in action. "Love one another as I have loved you!" (John 15:12), and again: "Greater love than this no one has than to lay down one's life for one's friends." (John 15:13) His love for us brought Him to death on a cross, even when we were still His enemies through sin. In a similar way we must be ready at all times to forget ourselves and to be concerned from the heart about the needs of our neighbor. This attitude of unselfish love and giving, of forgiving from our hearts, of caring for the other, must be carried into our daily living, beginning with our own immediate family members and then extending to everyone whose life we touch.

Homes are meant, in God's design, to be places of happy family life. How much unhappiness, how many quarrels, misunderstandings and heartaches could be avoided, and even marriages saved, if husbands and wives loved each other sincerely from the heart. Jesus invites us to learn from Him, because He is gentle and humble of Heart. (Matt. 11:29) In Scripture we find: "He opened not His mouth." (Is. 53:7) He did not repay insult with insult. For family members to hold back the sharp word, the insulting reproach, accusations which often end in serious offenses against love, is to imitate Jesus.

Open, honest, peaceful dialogue creates better understanding of each other's strengths and limitations. Each one discovers the beauty and preciousness of his God-given personality. Their privilege and duty is to help each other grow and to ever more fully become the persons God intends them to become. An atmosphere of family

prayer and sharing develops. Human and Christian at-
titudes will also then be transmitted to their children, who
must be taught early in their lives to become unselfish and
loving in their relationships with all family members.

In describing the quality our love ought to have, St.
Francis de Sales uses the concept *to love our neighbor with
the love of our heart*. He begins by saying love has its seat
in the heart. We find this identical expression used at the
very beginning of Christianity when St. Peter wrote his
first letter to the early Christians:

> By obedience to the truth you have purified yourselves for
> a genuine love of your brothers; therefore, love one
> another constantly from the heart. Your rebirth has come
> not from a destructible but from an indestructible seed,
> through the living and enduring word of God.
>
> (1 Peter 1:1-3)

> So strip away everything vicious, everything deceitful;
> pretenses, jealousies and disparaging remarks of any kind.
> Be eager for pure milk of the spirit to make you grow unto
> salvation, now that you have tasted that the Lord is
> good.'' (1 Peter 2:1-3)

This is a magnificent passage from the heart of Peter! It
expresses fully what our attitude toward each other ought
to be, as followers of the Lord. He also gives the reason
why we must love each other constantly from the heart. St.
Peter expresses here the great truth that through the grace
of our Baptism we have been purified of all sin. God's
own life has been poured into us, making us pure and holy.
It is this life, the life of the Heart of God in our own hearts,
which enables us to love one another constantly and genu-
nely from our hearts.

St. Peter calls this new life a rebirth which has come
from an indestructible seed, the living and enduring word
of God. We find this word of God in Scripture. If we

often read and ponder this word attentively and prayerfully, it will reveal to us how Jesus loves us constantly and genuinely from His Heart and how we can imitate Him effectively. Then all those things which injure or hurt or destroy this genuine love of neighbor in any way must be gotten rid of, relying not on ourselves but on the Lord who said: "Love one another as I have loved you." (John 15:12) "Learn of Me, for I am gentle and humble of Heart." (Matt. 11:29)

STRIVE AFTER PEACE

I saw a girl who carried a jug of water on her head.
  On the water swam a piece of wood.
    I asked why one does that.

To quiet the movement of the water,
  That nothing may be spilt, she answered.

In the same way, we ought to place
  The Cross into our hearts, so that
    Through this wood

The variations of our moods
  May be calmed.
Then they will not get caught up
  In any current of unrest. . .

Commentary

CROSSES [17]

St. Francis de Sales tells us that if we are to be happy in bearing the cross as well as profit from it, we must embrace it until we can lovingly fold it in our arms, or as we would familiarly say, hug it. By the closeness of our embrace we not only hold our treasure securely, but we also hide it within our arms and within our hearts.

Because of its priceless value, our Lord, through the cross, chose to purchase heaven for us, the only kingdom which will not pass away. In imitation of Him we must learn to cherish the cross, which will ready us to participate in His glorious Resurrection and in eternal happiness. In a letter of direction to a lady St. Francis de Sales expresses the following reflection:

> The cross is the royal road by which we enter the temple of Sanctity. He who seeks an entrance elsewhere will never find the smallest part of it. Love your cross well; it is all of gold if you look at it with eyes of love.
>
> (Letter MCMLXXXIII)

And again he writes:

> Be brave, take up your cross as if you and it were always to live in close companionship.

Casting a glance back on our own inner life, who of us can deny the healing qualities of the cross, its unfailing way of helping us by its deep touches to lead a happier and holier life?

To a lady of the French social world our Saint wrote these significant words:

> When we contemplate the blessed sign of our Redemption we recognize how wrong we are in giving to our trifling mishaps the name of afflictions. The lover of Christ Crucified makes a very jubilee, when by some slight participation he is allowed to share in it.

"These lessons," he says elsewhere, "are high lessons, but we learn them from the Most High." (Letter DLXII)

Other very wholesome lessons on suffering are contained in excerpts from letters written by our Saint to various persons:

> We give much stronger proof of our fidelity in suffering than in action. The martyrs are preferred to the confessors. You have a good exercise of mortification in being no longer able to sleep easily when lying down. Many of the saints practiced this mortification by choice. Now it is not of less value, but of more, when it is practiced by accepting it. The time of affliction is the true harvest time of real spiritual affections. (Letter DCCXXXI)

> Kiss in spirit the crosses our Lord places on your shoulders. Take no notice whether the wood of which they are made is precious or common. If the smell is offensive, they are all the truer crosses. Magdalen sought our Lord in the gardener's dress, and she continued to seek Him when He was already with her. Yet as soon as He said, 'Mary,' she recognized Him. When you meet our Lord here and there all day long in the ordinary mortifications that present themselves, you meet Him in the gardener's dress. What you would like is that He should offer you something more distinguished in the way of mortifications. My God! The grandest crosses are not the best. Before seeing Him in His glory He wants to plant in your garden many a lowly little flower to His own liking. That is why He comes to you in this guise. (Letter CDIV)

> You know that the fire which Moses saw on the mountain represented holy love. Just as its flames leaped up amid the thorns, so does the practice of sacred love maintain itself more happily amid tribulations than amid satisfactions.

> What a grace to be not only under, but on the Cross, and somewhat crucified with our Lord. Be of good courage and convert necessity into virtue. Do not lose the oppor-

tunity of bearing witness of your love for God amid tribulations, as He testified His love for us amid thorns.
(Letter CMLXIX)

Say often amid your contradictions: 'This is the very road to heaven. I see the door, and I am certain the storms cannot prevent us from getting there.' (Letter MCCLXXXI)

I see by your letters that you practice holy indifference in fact though not in feeling. This is a great subject of thanksgiving to God.

These little outbursts of passion of which you tell me are nothing. They are inevitable in this mortal life. 'Alas!' cries St. Paul, 'who will deliver me from the body of this death?'

We shall always feel the open or secret attacks of self-love, and if we do not wilfully and deliberately consent, that suffices. The virtue of indifference is so excellent that our human nature, according to its natural faculties, is incapable of it.

St. Francis then explains how our Lord as man was in no wise indifferent and did not desire to die on the cross. He continues:

Let us then remain in peace when we happen to violate the laws of indifference in indifferent matters, or, through sudden attacks of self-love or other passions. But let us turn to our Lord and make an act of trust and of humility, while peacefully and tranquilly we knot again the thread of our indifference and continue our work. We do not break the string or cast aside the lute when we perceive a discord, but bend our ear to find from where it comes and gently tighten or relax the string as required.
(Letter MDCLXXV)

The virtues which grow in the midst of prosperities are usually weak and without much backbone; but those which take birth amid afflictions are hardy and vigorous, just as it is said the best vines grow amid stones.

I pray God that He may always be in the midst of your heart, so that it may ever remain unshaken amid so many concussions, and that making you part of His Cross He will communicate to you His holy endurance, and give you that divine love which renders tribulations so precious.

(Letter MCMLXXIX)

The Cross is of God; but it is a cross because we do not unite ourselves to it, for when one is firmly resolved to will the cross that God sends, it is no longer a cross. It is only a cross because we do not will to have it. And if it is of God, why do we not will to have it? (Letter MMLXXX)

Not only in prayer time, but at all times, when you are going about, think over the pains of our Lord for our redemption and how blessed it is to participate in them. Think of the occasions when you may have an opportunity for this, such as the contradictions to your desires, and above all those desires which seem to you the most just and legitimate. Then, strong in your love of the Cross and Passion of our Lord, you will cry out with St. Andrew: 'O good Cross, so loved by my Saviour, when will you receive me into your arms.' (Letter DLXII)

May we meditate and contemplate often and deeply these invaluable lessons to become true lovers of our crucified Saviour!

"The fire of holy love which Moses saw on the mountain flamed up amid the thorns. So does the practice of sacred love maintain itself more happily amid tribulations."

St. Francis de Sales

Spiritual Directory

EVENNESS OF SPIRIT

Of inestimable value is the practice of the axiom:

ASK FOR NOTHING

AND

REFUSE NOTHING

Whatever is imposed upon us in the will of God,

we should take upon ourselves.

This also finds its expression in obedience.

In this surrender

is lodged peace and tranquillity of heart.

Selection from the Saint

SERENITY [18]

During this changeable life, one must preserve a steady and imperturbable evenness of spirit. Although everything may change around us, we must keep the serene glance of our soul constantly turned to God and our will ever attuned to His own good pleasure.

Selection from the Saint

SELF-FORGETFULNESS[19]

Be faithful and constant in your resolution to remain in simplicity in the presence of God. Abandon yourself completely to His holy will. Whenever you find your spirit outside this sphere, gently draw it back. Do not make any sensible acts of the understanding or of the will. This simple love and repose of your heart in the eternal bosom of our Lord and His Providence encompasses in an excellent manner all one could desire in order to be united with God.

Do not philosophize about your contradictions or afflictions. Accept all very simply, without exception, from the hand of God, recognizing His holy will. Let all your words and actions be accompanied by gentleness and simplicity. Remain in this holy solitude with our Crucified Lord. Return to the lovable purity of a child, so that our gentle Savior might take you up in His arms and carry you in His own way to the ultimate perfection of His love. Have courage! If God sometimes deprives you of the consolation and awareness of His presence, it is only that His presence itself might no longer occupy your heart, but He alone and His good pleasure. Those whose one desire is to please the Divine Lover have neither inclination nor leisure to turn back upon themselves. Their minds tend continually in the direction where love carries them.

God's heart so abounds in love, and His good is so great and infinite that everyone may possess it, while no one possesses less of it. God pours His love in no less measure into one soul, even though He loves an infinity of others along with it, than if He loved that soul alone.[20]

Chapter 6

CALVARY

Spiritual Directory

CALVARY IS THE MOUNT OF LOVE

Learn to accept that God can withdraw His felt nearness from us. The most difficult thing He requires of His friends is the renunciation, the demand not to despair of His eternal goodness, even when we feel forsaken by Him.

"Father, into your hands I commend my spirit." (Luke 23:46) When we have said this, what remains but to take the last breath and to die of love? We no longer live, but Christ lives in us.

Selection from the Saint

MOUNT CALVARY IS THE
TRUE SCHOOL OF LOVE[21]

Learn to distinguish between God and the feelings of God's nearness, between faith and the sentiment of faith. Not to perceive God's presence does not mean no longer walking in His presence. This would be unreasonable. While someone suffers a martyr's death for God, he possibly does not think about Him for a moment in his pains. Yet it is the highest love.

Everyone can easily trust in God during a time of peace and consolation. But surrendering to Him in trust when enduring trials, only those who are of His spirit are capable of this. However, God asks this of us. If we are able to receive it, we will be surprised to experience how, sooner or later, all fear from which our soul trembled will be dispelled.

Do not look forward to what might happen tomorrow; the same everlasting Father who cares for you today will take care of you tomorrow and every day. Either He will shield you from suffering, or He will give you unfailing strength to bear it. Be at peace then and put aside all anxious thoughts and imaginations.

God in His divine wisdom has from all eternity beheld the cross He bestows upon you — His precious gift from His Heart. He contemplated this cross with His all-knowing eye before giving it to you. He pondered it in His divine mind; he examined it in His all-wise justice; with His loving mercy He warmed it through and through; and with both His hands He weighed it to determine if it be one ounce too heavy for you. He blessed it with His all-holy Name; with His grace He anointed it; and with His consolation He perfumed it through and through; and then once more He considered you and your courage. Finally it comes from heaven as a special message of God to you, an alms of the all-merciful love of God for you.

The death and Passion of our Lord is the sweetest and most compelling motive that can animate our hearts in this mortal life. It is the very truth that mystical bees make their most excellent honey in the wounds of our Lord, who was slain and pierced upon Mount Calvary. The children of the Cross glory in this, their wondrous paradox, which the world does not understand: Out of death has come the food of our consolation and the honey of our love. [22]

Mount Calvary is the Mount of lovers. All love that does not take its origin from the Savior's Passion is foolish and perilous. Upon Calvary we cannot have life without love or love without the Redeemer's death. To die to all other loves that we may live in Your eternal love, O Savior of our souls, we eternally sing,

"LIVE ✝ JESUS"!

PART II

Additional Selections from the
Writings of

ST. FRANCIS DE SALES

for Health and Growth
in the Spiritual Life

Chapter 7

GOD'S ACTION UPON US

SPIRITUAL DIRECTION[23]

Do you wish to set out earnestly on the way to devotion? Seek out a good person to guide and help you. You will never find the will of God so surely as by seeking it through this way of mutual discernment, as did the devout men of old.

Pray earnestly for God to provide you with a Spiritual Director according to His heart, and have no doubt that even if He should have to send an angel from heaven, as He did to the young Tobias, He will give you one that is good and faithful.

Look upon this Spiritual Director not as a mere human being, nor trust in him or her as such, but in God, Who will favor you and speak to you through this person. The Holy Spirit will enable him or her to discern whatever you need for your happiness. Be open in all sincerity and fidelity, revealing clearly your strengths and limitations. Have the greatest confidence, mingled with reverence. This friendship must be strong, yet gentle, holy and spiritual, always rooted in God. This guide must be full of charity, knowledge and prudence. If one of these qualities is wanting, there is danger. Ask God to give you such a one, and bless and thank His goodness when you have found the right person.

METHOD FOR MEDITATION[24]

1. Before praying, choose one of the four ways of becoming aware of the presence of God, as shown in Part I, "Preparation for Meditation."

2. Even though you may feel a sense of unworthiness before God, know that His goodness desires you to adore Him. Make use of some short and ardent words from Sacred Scripture.

3. Imagine that the mystery upon which you are meditating is actually taking place before you. For example, if you wish to meditate on the crucifixion of our Lord, imagine it is taking place in the very spot where you are. As you advance in prayer, it would be better to make use of the simple thought of faith, and of an entirely spiritual apprehension within your own spirit.

4. Consider the mystery in order to stir up your affections toward God, to acquire virtue and to attain the love of God. Just as bees do not leave a flower as long as they find honey in it, so you remain with the consideration as long as it gives you spiritual nourishment. If not, pass to another quite gently and simply.

5. Then God will effect in you both love for Himself and your neighbor, a desire to imitate the life of our Lord, compassion, and confidence in God's goodness and mercy. Allow your spirit to expand and extend itself as much as possible by yielding to the movements of the Spirit of God. These inspirations will help you to make particular resolutions for your spiritual growth.

6. Close the meditation with acts of thanksgiving for the affections and resolutions God has given you. Offer

to Him the death and virtues of His Son, with petitions
for the Church and other intentions you may have.

7. Choose one or two points to which you were most attracted and which may help you grow spiritually.
Remember these throughout the day in order to practice
them carefully. This is the great fruit of meditation.
For example, I resolve to be gentle toward those who
offend me. When I meet them, I will be gracious. If I
do not meet them, I will speak well of them and pray
for them.

When you have finished this prayer of the heart,
take care not to become immediately too involved in
demanding work through which you may lose the feelings
and affections you have received. If possible, keep silence
for awhile and move quite gently from prayer to your occupations. If you converse with someone, for instance, do
so in such a way that you are also mindful of your heart,
so that the cordial of prayer may be spilled as little as
possible.

During vocal prayer, if you find your heart drawn
and invited to interior or mental prayer, don't refuse to
take it up. Let your mind turn very gently in that direction
and do not be concerned at not finishing the vocal prayers
you intended to say. The mental prayer you substitute for
them is more pleasing to God and more profitable for your
soul.

CONTEMPLATION [25]

Contemplation is simply the mind's loving, undivided, permanent attention to the things of God. When meditation produces devotion, it becomes contemplation. We meditate to be filled with the love of God. After receiving this love, we contemplate Him and are attentive to His goodness, because of the delight and love we find in Him. This love is at last crowned with perfection when it possesses what it loves.

In order to love, knowledge is necessary. We can never love a thing we do not know. In this life, however, we can have greater love than knowledge of God. Brother Giles, one of St. Francis' first companions, said one day to St. Bonaventure, "O, how happy you learned men are! You understand many things by which you praise God; but what can we simple fellows do?" St. Bonaventure replied, "The grace to be able to serve God is sufficient." "But, my Father," answered Brother Giles, "can an ignorant man love God as much as a learned man?" "He can," the Saint replied, "and furthermore, a poor, simple woman can love God as much as a doctor of divinity!"

Faith assures us of the infinite good which is in God and, so, gives us sufficient reason to love Him with all our power. We begin to love by the knowledge faith gives us of God's goodness. Then we savor and taste this love. It is as divine wisdom has said, "They that taste Me shall yet hunger and they that drink Me shall thirst for more." Knowledge is not contrary to devotion, but very useful to it. When joined together, they wonderfully help each other.

Contemplation always has this special quality, that it is made with delight. It presupposes that we have found

God and His love and that we find joy and delight in Him, for we say, "I have found Him Whom my soul loves, I will not let Him go." (Cant. 3:4) Contemplation raises us above ourselves, so that we may live more in God than in ourselves. All our attention is centered in seeing His beauty and being united with His goodness.

To attain to contemplation we must read Sacred Scripture, take part in spiritual discussions with others, read good books, pray, meditate and think good thoughts. Contemplation is the end to which all these exercises tend.

LOVING RECOLLECTION
IN CONTEMPLATION[26]

The recollection I speak of is given by God Himself. It is not within our power to have it when we will, nor does it depend on our own efforts. At His own pleasure God works in us.

It takes place in this way. In an imperceptible manner our Lord sometimes infuses into our hearts a certain tender feeling that bears witness to His presence. We then turn toward our center where He is. At such a time He pours into our hearts consolations, through which we rest in Him as in our greatest good. "O God," says the soul in imitation of St. Augustine, "where did I go in search for You, O Infinite Beauty? I sought You outside myself, and You were in the midst of my heart."

When our Lady had conceived the Son of God, her soul was completely centered upon that beloved Child. This same contentment may be attained by those who have received Holy Communion and who with sure faith feel that which "neither flesh nor blood," but the heavenly Father has revealed to them. Their hearts and all their faculties are drawn together to adore their Lord present in their inmost being. They receive unbelievable spiritual consolation and refreshment in knowing by faith He is present within them. Note carefully, this recollection is wholly produced by love.

This sweet recollection of our soul is made not only by knowledge of God's presence within our heart, but also by any way of placing ourselves in His sacred presence. The beloved St. John, when resting on his Master's bosom at the Last Supper, undoubtedly fell into a mystical sleep. Sometimes this repose goes so deep in its tranquillity that the whole soul and all its powers remain as if sunk in sleep. They make no movement or action whatever, except the will alone, even if it does no more than receive the joy and contentment the Beloved's presence gives it. What is more wonderful still is that the will does not perceive the joy it receives, but enjoys it insensibly. It does not think of itself, but of Him whose presence gives it such pleasure.

When you are in this state of simple, pure, filial confidence with our Lord, remain there without moving yourself to make conscious acts, either of understanding or of will. This simple, trustful love and loving rest of your spirit in the arms of the Savior supremely contains all that you seek, now here now there, to satisfy your desires. It is better to rest there than to be awake elsewhere, no matter where it may be.

Tell me, I ask you, should a soul recollected in its God disturb itself? Does it not have cause to be at peace and to remain in repose? For what would it seek? It has found Him Whom it seeks. It has no further need to trouble itself with intellectual discussions. By a single glance it sees that its Beloved is present and all reasoning would be unprofitable and superfluous. Even if the soul does not see Him with the intellect, it is content to feel His nearness by the delight and satisfaction the will receives. When our Lady neared her time, she did not see her divine Child but felt Him within her sacred womb. O God, what joy she experienced! And St. Elizabeth, did she not rejoice in a wondrous way and recognize our Savior's divine presence on the day of the Visitation, even though she did not see Him? In such repose the soul has no further need of memory or imagination, for its Lover is present with it. The will alone draws in gently this sweet presence while the soul remains in quiet.

There is a great difference between being occupied with God, Who gives us this contentment, and concerning ourselves with the contentment God gives to us. The soul whom God favors with this loving quietude must not regard either itself or its repose. To be guarded, this repose must not be regarded. The one who loves it too much loses it.

Sometimes the soul not only perceives the presence of God, but hears Him speak by certain inward lights and persuasions which take the place of words. Sometimes it perceives Him speaking and in turn it speaks to Him, but so secretly, so delicately, that there is no loss of holy peace and quiet. The soul watches and speaks with its Beloved, heart to heart, with such gracious repose that it is as if the soul slumbered.

There are times when the soul neither hears its Beloved nor speaks to Him, nor does it feel any sign of His presence. It simply knows that it is in God's presence, to Whom it is pleasing that the soul is there. For instance, we look at Him or at something out of love for Him, we listen to Him or to those who speak for Him; we speak to Him or to someone out of love for Him; or we do some work, no matter what it may be, for His honor and His service. Or again, we do none of these things, but remain simply where it pleases Him for us to be and because it pleases Him that we are there. If to this He adds some slight perception that we are all His and He is all ours, then how desirable and precious is our grace!

How excellent is this way of keeping in God's presence, so as to be and to wish always and forever to be at His good pleasure! It is such because it is free from any kind of self-interest. To conclude, the height of loving ecstasy is when our will rests not in its own contentment, but in God's will.

Chapter 8

OUR COOPERATION
WITH GOD'S ACTION

DIVINE GIFTS[27]

When charity enters a heart it brings with it all the other virtues or divine gifts. However, we must not practice them all at once, but discern which are appropriate.

There are few opportunities to practice fortitude, magnanimity, or magnificence. But whatever we do should be colored with gentleness, temperance, modesty and humility. There are gifts from God which are more excellent, but the practice of these is more important. We must use them almost continually.

Among the divine gifts we should prefer those which are most conformable to our duty and not most to our liking. For example, King St. Louis visited hospitals and served the sick with his own hands. St. Francis loved poverty, which he called his lady. St. Gregory the Great took pleasure in entertaining pilgrims. St. Elizabeth, though a great princess, delighted in nothing as much as working among the poor in a spirit of self-forgetfulness. The Saints excelled in various virtues in imitation of our Lord.

Job, by practicing great patience during so many temptations, became perfectly holy. As St. Gregory of Nazianzen says, by a single act of some divine gift well and perfectly used, we may attain to the height of virtue. We, too, when assailed by pride or anger ought to incline and bend ourselves toward humility and gentleness, as did Job. Also our exercises of prayer and of the Sacraments ought to tend to this end.

Let us practice patience, meekness, mortification of the heart, humility, obedience, poverty, chastity, consideration for others, bearing with their imperfections, diligence, and holy fervor. However, we should not aspire to ecstasies or raptures which are not virtues, but rather rewards which God gives for virtue. These graces are not at all necessary for true service and love of God. If we stay humbly in our way, which is lower but safer and more suited to our littleness, God will raise us to grandeurs which are great indeed.

PATIENCE [28]

The more perfect our patience is, the more perfectly do we possess our souls. To possess our souls is our greatest happiness. Often call to mind that our Lord saved us by suffering and enduring. We also must work out our salvation by afflictions, enduring injuries, contradictions and troubles with as much sweetness as we can.

Let us not limit our patience to certain afflictions, but extend it universally to all those which God may permit to happen. Some are willing to suffer honorable tribulations, such as being wounded in battle or ill-treated for religion. But a true servant of God also bears those which are accompanied by ignominy. The evil we receive at the hands of good men is much harder to bear than from others. I think more of the meekness with which the great St. Charles Borromeo suffered the public rebukes of a great preacher for a long time, than of the patience with which he bore all the attacks he received from others.

Complain as little as possible of the wrongs which are done to you. Ordinarily he who complains sins, because self-love makes us think the injuries greater than they are. If you must make known your hurt to someone, choose a peaceable person and one who loves God, so that your heart may be eased instead of provoked to greater disturbance.

When you are sick, afflicted or offended by anyone, do not look for sympathy and compassion. This is a false patience, a very subtle ambition and vanity. The truly patient person does not complain or seek sympathy. He or she speaks of it unaffectedly, truthfully and simply.

When you are sick, offer all your sufferings, pains and weariness to the service of our Lord and ask Him to unite them to those which He suffered for you. Obey the physician. Take the medicines for the love of God, to be cured in order to serve Him. To obey Him, do not refuse to be ill; also, be prepared to die if He should will it. Remember that the bees eat a very bitter food when they make honey. In the same way, we can never perform actions of greater gentleness and patience, nor better produce the honey of excellent virtues, than while eating the bitter bread of afflictions.

Look often with your interior eyes upon our Lord crucified, naked, blasphemed and abandoned, and know that all your sufferings are not to be compared with His, either in quality or in quantity. You will never suffer anything for Him which can be compared with what He has suffered for you.

HUMILITY [29]

Humility preserves in us the graces and gifts of the Holy Spirit. In order to prepare for this, we must be empty of self.

We call that glory vain which we give to ourselves. For example, sometimes we praise ourselves for that which is not in us or for that which is in us, but is not ours. At other times we praise ourselves for that which is in us and is ours, but does not deserve we should glory in it. To know whether someone is truly wise, learned, generous and great, we must see if the good things in him or her tend to humility, modesty and submission. True balm is tested by dropping it into water. If it goes to the bottom and takes the lowest place, it is judged to be the finest and the most precious. Beauty, to have real charm, should be unaffected. Knowledge ought not to puff us up, for then it discredits us. They that aspire to virtue are not eager for honor and status. Everyone may take the place due to him and keep it without prejudice to humility, provided it is done unaffectedly and without contention.

What I have said so far is rather wisdom than humility. I will now pass on further. Many will not consider the graces which God has bestowed upon them personally, being afraid of vainglory and self-complacency. In this they deceive themselves. To truly attain to the love of God we must consider his benefits, especially those bestowed on us personally, since these move us more powerfully.

We need not fear that the knowledge of what God has placed in us will puff us up, provided we are attentive to this truth, that what is good in us is not of ourselves, but His gift. The lively consideration of the graces we have received makes us humble. Knowledge begets acknowl-

edgment. If we remember what we have done when God
has not been with us, we shall realize clearly that what we
do when He is with us is not our own doing or thinking.
We shall indeed possess the good and we shall rejoice
because we possess it, but we shall give the glory to God
alone, because He is the author of it. The Blessed Virgin
confesses that God has done great things for her, but it is
only to humble herself, and to magnify God. "My soul,"
she says, "magnifies the Lord, because He has done great
things for me."

True humility makes no pretense of being humble
and scarcely ever speaks words of humility, for it desires
not only to hide the other virtues, but principally it seeks
to hide itself.

Some say they leave mental prayer to the perfect or
they dare not receive the Eucharist often. Others fear to
disgrace devotion if they meddle with it, or they refuse to
employ their talents in the service of God and their
neighbor. They say they know their feebleness and are
afraid of becoming proud. Under pretext of humility they
conceal the love of their own opinion, inclination and
slothfulness. They excuse themselves from aspiring to the
grace to which the divine goodness invites them. When
God wishes to bestow some favor upon us, it is pride to
refuse. The gifts of God oblige us to receive them. It is
humility to obey and to follow as closely as we can His
desires. The more humble persons realize their weakness.
In the light of this knowledge they become more courageous, placing all their confidence in God. He is pleased
to magnify His power in our weakness and to manifest His
mercy in our misery. We must, therefore, dare with humble confidence all that is proper for our progress.

Moreover, when charity requires it, we must freely

and gently impart to our neighbor what is necessary for his instruction and consolation. For humility, which hides and covers virtues to preserve them, causes them nevertheless to appear at charity's command, to develop, increase and perfect them.

GENTLENESS[30]

The chrism which is used for Confirmation and con-
secrations is composed of olive oil mingled with balm.
This represents the two virtues of the Heart of our Lord
which He has particularly recommended to us when He
said: "Learn of me, for I am meek and humble of heart."
(Matt. 11:29) Humility perfects us in regard to God, and
gentleness, in regard to our neighbor. The balm, which as
I have said above always sinks to the bottom, represents
humility. The olive oil, which always floats on top,
represents gentleness. But take care that this chrism com-
pounded of gentleness and humility be within your heart.
There are many who appear to possess these divine gifts or
imagine they are humble and gentle, but in reality they are
not. Such persons, at the least petty injury they receive,
start up with great arrogance. This is a sign their humility
and gentleness are not true and sincere, but artificial.

If you can possibly help it, do not be angry at all
under any pretext whatever, but journey onwards with
your companions gently, peaceably and amicably. As St.
Augustine says, "It is better to deny admittance to just
anger, because once it enters, it is difficult to make it
depart." When you experience the first movement of
anger you must promptly collect your forces, not roughly
but gently, so that you may not be more disturbed. Then
ask our Lord to help you, as the Apostles did, to calm the
storm.

Moreover, when you commit an act of anger, repair
the fault promptly by an act of gentleness toward the same
person. In addition, when you are without any occasion
to anger, lay up a great store of gentleness and meekness.
Speak all your words and perform all your actions,

whether small or great, as gently as you possibly can. (St. Francis de Sales, being of a choleric temperament, overcame himself so well that it was said of him he was like our Savior walking again on this earth.)

We must not only be gentle and meek toward others, but above all, toward ourselves. We must not fret over our own imperfections. After committing a fault, never give into bitter, gloomy or spiteful regret or displeasure. It is self-love which causes us to be disturbed and upset when we see we are imperfect. Our sorrow must be calm, firm and settled. A father's gentle, loving rebuke has far greater power to correct a child than rage and passion. Let us then be mild and compassionate toward ourselves, and remain humbly before God, so that our repentance may be sincere and from the heart.

OBEDIENCE [31]

Charity alone places us in perfection, but obedience, chastity and poverty are the three great means of acquiring it. Obedience consecrates our heart, chastity, our body and poverty, our possessions to the love and service of God. To render us perfect we need only to observe these virtues.

There are two states of obedience, the one necessary, the other voluntary. We must obey our ecclesiastical, our political and our household superiors, since God has placed them over us. To be perfect, follow their counsels and even their desires and inclinations, as far as charity and prudence permit. Obey in indifferent things as well as when a difficult or unpleasant duty is requested. Obey lovingly for love of Him Who became obedient unto death of the cross, for love of you.

In order to learn readily to obey your superiors, comply readily with the will of your equals, yielding to their opinions without contradicting. Accommodate yourself willingly to the desires of your inferiors without exercising any imperious authority over them, so long as they are good.

There is also a voluntary obedience to which those bind themselves who choose to obey a Spiritual Director. The works of piety performed through this obedience are more pleasing to God. Blessed are the obedient, for God will never suffer them to go astray.

Commentary on *"Obedience"*

What a challenge St. Francis de Sales presents to us in the practice of obedience! He explains:

> Charity alone places us in perfection, but obedience is one of the three great means of acquiring it. Obedience consecrates our heart to the love and service of God. To render us perfect, obedience is one of the virtues we must observe.

Francis uses a beautiful analogy of the sunflower to illustrate how our will should be constantly attracted by the divine will.

> Just as the sunflower turns its flowers and all its leaves to the sun, we, by obedience to the commandments, turn our hearts to the divine will. However, those entirely caught up in God's love follow the divine will in all it commands, counsels and inspires them to do. This is the way in which our hearts grow in likeness to the heart of God. God's supreme goodness and excellence of perfection merit that we unite our will to His in loving obedience.
> (*Treatise on the Love of God,* Book 8, Chapter 2)

Let us now look at the expression of God's will in our lives. When God sends His inspiration into someone's heart, the first one He gives is that of obedience. St. Francis de Sales is strong on the concept that union with the will of God is union with the will of our neighbor. He holds up to us the story of the conversion of St. Paul. Ananias was sent by the Lord to Paul to make known to him what He wanted him to do. This manner of revealing His will through other human beings has been God's method throughout the history of His Chosen People. He has not changed His ways in our own time. When we, in our daily personal interactions in family and religious life, are attuned to each other with an open mind and a listening heart, God's will can be more easily disclosed to us in our lives.

In a conference "On Obedience" St. Francis de Sales writes:

> Obedience is so excellent a virtue that our Lord condescended to direct the whole course of His life on earth by it. Jesus came not to do His own will, but the will of His Father. (John 4:34) In St. Paul's letter to the Philippians we read, 'He made Himself obedient unto death, even death on a cross.' (Phil. 2:8) Jesus was pleased to add to the infinite merits of His perfect charity the infinite merits of a perfect obedience.
>
> (Book of Conferences)

CHASTITY [32]

Chastity implies integrity. It is the beautiful and white virtue of the soul and of the body. While charity is the queen of the virtues, chastity is the lily of the virtues.

Everyone has great need of this gift from God. Widowed persons must have a courageous chastity. Virgins have need of an extremely simple and delicate chastity. Never doubt that this virtue is incomparably better than anything that is incompatible with it. It is also very necessary for married people to practice this virtue.

"Follow peace with everyone," says the Apostle, "and holiness, without which no one shall see God." The holiness which he means is chastity, for our Savior Himself said, "Blessed are the clean of heart, for they shall see God." (Matt. 5:8)

Keep yourself always close to Jesus Christ crucified, both spiritually by meditation, and really by Holy Communion, resting your heart upon Him Who is the immaculate Lamb.

POVERTY[33]

"Blessed are the poor in spirit, for theirs is the kingdom of heaven." (Matt. 5:3)

I would place into your heart both riches and poverty together, a great care of temporal things, as well as a great disregard for them. To possess riches, but to be poor in affection for them, is the great happiness of the Christian.

Do not place your spirit within earthly goods, but be always master of them. Use them wisely and well, that they may be fruitful and that they may be increased for the glory of God, because they are not your own. Cultivate them and make them profitable with a gentle care, since God Who gave them to you, wills that you should do so for love of Him.

Unless we practice some real and effective poverty in the midst of the possessions God has given us, self-love can lead us to greed. It is a good practice to always deprive ourselves of part of what we own, in order that we might give to the poor with a willing heart. There is nothing that makes a person prosper as much as almsgiving, for God will bless this generosity abundantly, both in this life and in the next.

Love the poor and poverty, for by this love you will become truly poor in spirit. If you love the poor, be often among them, visit them and willingly associate with them. Be glad that they are near you in the churches, in the streets and elsewhere.

Will you do even more? Then do not be content with desiring to be poor, but become a servant of the poor through your availability, love and concern for them. This service has more glory in it than a throne, for our Lord said, "I was hungry and you gave me to eat, I was naked and you clothed me, I was sick and in prison and you visited me. Possess the kingdom prepared for you from the foundation of the world." (Matt. 25:35, 36)

Accept with a willing heart whatever inconveniences and misfortunes come your way and suffer them cheerfully. If you are concerned with caring for your possessions because God has given them to you, you will not lose your peace of soul when He permits them to be taken away.

If you are really poor, have patience. You are in good company. Our Lord, Our Lady, the Apostles and so many saints, who could have been rich, chose to live in poverty. Poverty came to you without your seeking it. Embrace it then, as the dear friend of our Lord.

The first privilege of your poverty is that it did not come to you by your own choice, but by the will of God alone. What we receive purely from the will of God, provided we do so with a willing heart and for love of Him, is always very pleasing to Him. This simple and entire acceptance of the will of God makes suffering extremely pure.

The second privilege of this kind of poverty is that it is authentically poor. If poverty displeases you, you are not poor in spirit. To desire to be poor, but not to be inconvenienced by it, is a great ambition. Make, therefore, a virtue out of necessity.

Treasure the gift God has placed into your hands in the form of actual poverty. Set a high value on so precious a gem, which is not appreciated by the world, but is exceedingly beautiful in the eyes of God.

Often call to mind the journey of Our Lady to Egypt. Think of how much contempt, poverty and misery she had to endure. If you imitate this way, you will be rich in your poverty.

SIMPLICITY³⁴

Since the virtue of simplicity is a very necessary one, we ought to understand what it is. It can be defined as an act of pure and simple charity which has only one aim, that of loving God. Our soul is simple when in all we do or desire we have no other goal. This divine gift will admit of no self-interest, for God alone finds place in it.

Our Lord Himself made the virtue of simplicity known to us when He said to His Apostles, "Be wise as serpents, but simple as doves." Learn from the dove to love God in singleness of heart. Imitate not only the simple love of these birds who do everything for their one mate, but also the simplicity with which they express their love. They do not practice little cunning ways, but only coo gently and are happy just to rest quietly in the presence of their mate.

There are many who, with solicitous care, seek out various exercises and means to love God. It is quite impossible for them to be at peace. They torment themselves about finding the art of loving God, not knowing there is none, except to love Him. They think a certain method is needed to acquire this love, but it is to be found only in simplicity.

This divine gift embraces all the necessary means to acquire the love of God in one's vocation. But the reason must be without any other consideration. For simplicity cannot bear to concern itself about anything, however perfect, except to love God purely.

Moreover, simplicity is not contrary to prudence. The virtues never clash with each other, but are bound together in closest union. This virtue is opposed to cunning, which causes deceit and duplicity. These in turn lead us to try to convince our neighbor that there is no other feeling in our heart but what is expressed in our words. This is absolutely contrary to simplicity, which requires that the interior should wholly conform to the exterior.

When, however, our emotions are inwardly disturbed, we ought not to make an outward demonstration of them. It is not contrary to simplicity to show a calm exterior at such times. We may be much disturbed by a reproof or a contradiction, but this upset does not proceed from our will. All the trouble goes on in the lower part of our soul. The higher does not consent, but accepts and values the contradiction. The love of God requires us, after having owned our feelings, to restrain them.

Are we deceiving those who see us and who think we are virtuous, when we are really unmortified? Reflection about what others think or say of us is contrary to simplicity. After the simple soul has done any action it considers it ought to do, it thinks no more about the matter. The soul will suffer nothing to distract it from its one aim, to dwell on the thought of God alone, that it may love Him more and more.

Your well-being depends on your allowing yourself to be guided and governed by the Spirit of God without reserve. This is the aim of that true simplicity which our Lord recommends so highly. He says to His Apostles, "Unless you become simple as little children, you cannot enter the kingdom of heaven." (Matt. 18:3)

The soul which has attained perfect simplicity has only one love, which is for God. In this love it has only one aim — to rest upon the bosom of the heavenly Father. There, like a loving child, it leaves all care of self to that good Father, anxious about nothing, except to live in this confidence. It is not even disquieted by any desire for virtues which seem necessary to it. Such a soul, it is true, uses every opportunity for doing good which it meets with on the way, but it does not anxiously hunt about for means of perfecting itself.

This exercise of continued self-abandonment into the hands of God, encompasses the perfection of all other exercises in its absolute simplicity and purity. While God leaves us the use of it, we ought not to change it.

Chapter 9

COUNSELS

TEMPTATIONS[35]

There are three steps in temptations:

1. Sin is proposed to the soul.
2. The soul is pleased or displeased with the suggestions.
3. Finally, it consents or refuses.

Even though the temptation to any sin whatsoever snould last all our life, it cannot render us displeasing to God, provided we do not take pleasure in it or consent to it. St. Paul suffered temptations of the flesh for a long time and glorified God thereby. Blessed Angela of Foligno, St. Francis and St. Benedict likewise endured great temptations which did not diminish the grace of God in them, but greatly augmented it.

We must be very courageous in the midst of temptations. Never judge ourselves overcome as long as they displease us. Note carefully the difference between feeling temptations and consenting to them. We cannot consent to them unless we take pleasure in them. It is not possible to offend God as long as we are resolved not to take pleasure in them. Although it is not always possible for the soul not to feel the temptation, it is always in its power to reject it.

Amid great temptations charity, which is our spiritual life, seems reduced to a very small dimension. It appears to be only in the very center of the heart. Indeed, it seems not to even be there, and it is difficult to discover it at all. But charity is truly there, since, even though all may be troubled in our soul and in our body, we have resolved not to consent to the temptation. Although it is all about our will, yet it is not within it and being such, cannot be sin.

The best way to overcome both small and great temptations is to turn your heart simply to Jesus Christ crucified and, by an act of love, kiss His sacred feet. The love of God, containing in itself all the perfections of all the virtues, is also a supreme remedy against all the vices. Your soul will accustom itself to seek calm in this great protection. The evil spirit will cease to trouble you.

Finally, consider from time to time what passions are predominant in your soul. Make many acts of the contrary virtue, in order to strengthen your heart against future temptations.

DISQUIETUDE[36]

Disquietude is not a mere temptation, but a source from which and through which many temptations come. Sadness is sorrow of heart which we feel when we experience some exterior ill, such as poverty, sickness, contempt; or some interior suffering, such as dryness, repugnance or temptation. The soul desires to be delivered. If it seeks the means to accomplish this for the love of God, it will do so with patience, gentleness, humility and tranquillity. It will expect deliverance more from the goodness and providence of God, than from its own labors or diligence. If it acts from motives of self-love, it will be eager and heated, behaving as if more depended upon itself than upon God.

Disquietude is the greatest evil that can come upon a soul, except sin. The heart, when troubled and disquieted, loses its power to maintain the virtues it has acquired and also the strength to resist the enemy, who makes every effort to fish in troubled waters.

When you desire greatly to be delivered from some ill, or to obtain some good, place your spirit in repose and tranquillity. Compose your judgment and your will. Then, quite gently and quietly, pursue the object you desire, using the proper means in an orderly manner.

Examine more than once every day whether your heart is in your hands, or whether it is entangled in some passion of love, hatred, envy, covetousness, fear or joy. If it has wandered, bring it back quite gently to the presence of God. Subject your affections and desires to the direction of the divine will.

Do not allow your desires, however small and unimportant they may be, to disquiet you, for after the little ones, the greater and more important desires would find your heart more disposed to trouble and disorder. Recommend yourself to God when you experience disquietude. Resolve to act gently, moderating the course of your desire as much as you can. Act according to reason, not according to your desire.

Make known your disquietude to him who directs you, or to a faithful friend, and be assured that you will at once find relief.

SADNESS [37]

The enemy takes advantage of sadness to tempt the good. He strives to make them sorrowful in their good works, since he is sad and melancholy himself.

Evil sadness leads the soul into disquietude, inordinate fears, and distaste for prayer. It dulls and oppresses the brain, deprives the soul of counsel, of resolution, of judgment, of courage, and weakens its energy. It takes away all sweetness from the soul and makes it almost paralyzed, powerless in all its faculties.

If you ever find yourself sad, use the following remedies:

1) Pray. Prayer lifts the soul to God, Who is our consolation. But when you pray, use aspirations and words which tend to confidence in God and to love of Him.

2) Resist inclination to sadness with determination. Though it may seem to you that whatever is done at such a time is done coldly and half-heartedly, do not omit these good works, since then they become more meritorious.

3) Sing spiritual hymns and songs to resist the evil one. The violence of Saul's evil spirit was repressed by music.

4) Occupy yourself with exterior works. Vary these as much as possible to divert yourself from what causes the sadness and to purify and warm the spirit.

5) Receive Holy Communion. This is an excellent remedy. This heavenly bread strengthens

the heart and rejoices the spirit.

6) Make known all the feelings, affections and suggestions that arise from sadness to your Director, humbly and faithfully. Seek the company of spiritual persons and be with them as much as you can during such times.

7) Resign yourself patiently into the hands of God, not doubting at all, that after He has proved you, He will deliver you from sadness.

SPIRITUAL CONSOLATIONS[38]

It is important to maintain evenness of spirit although everything turns upside down, not only around us, but even within us. Whether we are in light or darkness, in peace or anxiety, in dryness or consolation, in sweetness or bitterness, in sadness or joy, we must keep our eyes fixed on God and aspire toward Him.

True and solid devotion consists in a constant, resolute, prompt and active will to do what we know is pleasing to God. There is no doubt but that His consolations stimulate the soul, strengthen the spirit, and add joy and cheerfulness to devotion. These make our actions beautiful and agreeable, even exteriorly. If these feelings of sweetness and consolation make us more humble, patient, charitable and compassionate towards our neighbor, more zealous to mortify our evil inclinations, more docile and obedient, more simple in our lives, there can be no doubt they come from God. On the contrary, if we become inquisitive, impatient, stubborn, proud or hard towards our neighbor, imagining we are already little saints, there is reason to believe they are false.

When we receive such consolations we must accept these graces and favors humbly and value them very highly, because it is God who infuses them into our hearts. We must use them carefully, according to His intention, that is, to make us gentle towards others and loving towards Him. We must, however, be willing to relinquish consolations at God's good pleasure.

SPIRITUAL DRYNESS [39]

Consolations, which are so pleasant, will not last always. Sometimes you will be so deprived of all feelings of devotion that your soul will seem to you to be a barren desert without any road to find God, or any water of grace to water it. The soul in this state does indeed deserve compassion.

What is to be done during such a time? Try to find the cause of this evil. Often we bring dryness upon ourselves.

Consider some reasons why God may withdraw His consolations from us:

1. When we take vain complacency in them.
2. When we neglect to gather the sweetness and delight of the love of God when it is time to do so.
3. When we are unwilling to give up vain amusements and false contentments to the detriment of our spiritual exercises.
4. When we are insincere in our confessions and communications with our Director.
5. When we fill ourselves with worldly pleasures.
6. When, through our own fault, we do not carefully preserve the fruit of consolation already received.

In the light of these reasons examine quietly whether the cause of the evil is in yourself. If so, thank God for this discovery, for an evil is half cured when one finds the cause. If, on the contrary, you see nothing in particular, then very simply do what I suggest.

1. Humble yourself deeply before God, conscious of your helplessness and nothingness.

2. Ask God for His joy and consolations.

3. Open your heart to your Confessor. Allow him to see clearly all the recesses of your soul. Follow his counsels with great simplicity and humility. God, who loves obedience, often makes the counsels profitable which we take from our Spiritual Director, even though they may not seem likely to be helpful.

4. Make use of types of prayer which may rekindle your fervor and help you to surrender to the Lord, such as charismatic prayer, centering prayer and prayer of the heart.

   a) Charismatic prayer, in which you praise and thank God and implore the love and gifts of the Spirit, may touch your heart and lift up your own spirit.

   b) Centering prayer. As you slowly repeat your favorite words, such as "Jesus," or "My Jesus Mercy," or any other short aspiration you may choose, you will be strengthened and enabled to surrender to His love.

   c) Prayer of the heart disposes you to express in short, but fervent aspirations, your love for God, Who lives within you. From it you will receive courage to persevere.

5. Extra bodily rest and some relaxation may be a real source of re-creating and renewing the spirit at the same time.

6. Give yourself generously to others in works of charity and of mercy. This will dispose you to forget your own suffering and to draw down upon yourself God's bountiful compassion.

It is of great value, however, to have no attachment to the desire of being delivered from this dryness. Resign yourself to the mercy of the particular providence of God and allow Him to make use of you in the midst of these deserts, as long as it pleases Him. When God sees you in this holy indifference, He will console you with many graces and favors.

Finally, do not lose courage in dryness. Always pursue exercises of devotion, multiply good works and offer to God a heart perfectly steadfast in its will to love Him. In this way you will abound in the practice of solid and true virtues — patience, humility, resignation and abnegation of self-love.

It is a great mistake to think our service of God is less agreeable to Him when made amid dryness. On the contrary, the value in His eyes becomes greater, since our will then carries us by main force and consequently is more vigorous and constant, than in times of consolation. Therefore, our perseverence is a true sign of fidelity and constancy, and of the purity of divine love in our hearts.

DESIRES[40]

The Lord taught me from my youth to trust Him. If I came into this world again, I would let Him lead me in the most insignificant matters, with the simplicity of a child and with disdain of all human prudence.

To wish to be in another state or calling taps the energies of the heart and makes it weak in carrying out our necessary duties. Do not desire to have greater talents or better judgment, but cultivate your own gifts, such as they are. Rather than desire other means of serving God, make good use of those you have. However, simple wishes do no harm, provided that they are not frequent.

Do not desire crosses, except in proportion to the measure with which you have borne those already sent you. It is an illusion to desire martyrdom and not to have the courage to bear an injury. The evil spirit often suggests such desires to divert our minds from present happenings, through which we might grow spiritually. Do not be rash and desire temptations, but prepare your heart for them, and defend yourself from them when they come.

Among so many desires, choose, with the advice of your Spiritual Director, those which can be practiced in the present. When you have done this, God will send you others which you will also carry out in good time. I do not say that we should ever lose good desires of any kind. But we must practice them in order. Those which cannot be carried out immediately must be locked away in our hearts until their opportune time comes. If we do this, we will enjoy peace of soul.

THE WILL OF GOD [41]

The determination to follow the will of God in all things, without exception, is contained in the *Lord's Prayer* in these words we repeat every day: "Your will be done on earth as it is in Heaven." (Matt. 6:10) In Heaven there is no resistance to the will of God. We ask our Lord to grant us the same grace, never to oppose the divine will in the slightest, but to be absolutely obedient to it on all occasions. Those who do this need to discern how they may recognize God's will.

The divine will may be understood in two ways:

1. God's declared will, namely, the Commandments of God and of the Church, the evangelical counsels and inspirations.

Everyone must obey the Commandments, because this is the absolute will of God. We do not lose charity or separate ourselves from God, if we lack courage to undertake the evangelical counsels. We ought only to practice those which are suitable to our vocation and not imagine He wants us to embrace them all.

God also reveals His will to us by His inspirations. He desires that in all matters of importance in which we cannot clearly see what we ought to do, we discern with those He has given us as guides about whatever concerns the perfection of our souls. This is the way God manifests His known will to us.

2. There is also the will of God's good pleasure.

This will of God we must regard in all the events and circumstances that may befall us. In sickness and in death, in affliction and consolation, in adversity and prosperity, in all the unforeseen occurrences of life, we must always be ready to submit to this will of God, whether the thing pleases us or not.

How worthy of love is this divine will! A law that is all of love and all for love! The soul that loves God is so transformed into the divine will that it merits to be described as the will of God, rather than as obedient and subject to it.

In the life of St. Anselm we read how greatly he was loved by all because he so readily condescended and yielded to the will of his monks and strangers. When questioned about this he explained, he could not discover God's good pleasure more certainly than through the voice of his neighbor.

> God commands me to show charity to my neighbor. It is great charity to live in harmony with one another. I find no better means than by being gentle and considerate. My chief reason, however, is that I believe God manifests His will to me through my brothers. Therefore, every time I comply with their wishes in anything I am obeying Him.

UNION OF OUR WILL WITH
GOD'S GOOD PLEASURE[42]

God in His great goodness distributes many different favors to everyone. He also deals out justly an infinite variety of trials.

Since the effects of His justice are severe and bitter, God sweetens them in His mercy. Death, afflictions, poverty, hunger, thirst, sorrow, sickness, persecution, sweat and toil, with which life abounds, are by His just decree punishments for the sins of mankind. But they are also by His kind mercy ladders to ascend to heaven, means to increase in grace, and merits to obtain glory.

Let us turn to ourselves in particular and see all that divine providence has prepared for us. Opening the arms of our consent, let us lovingly embrace all this as we make God's holy will our own. "Your will be done, on earth as it is in Heaven." (Matt. 6:10) Yes, Lord, Your will be done on earth where we have no pleasure without some pain, no day without a night to follow, where consolations are rare and trials are countless. Nevertheless, may Your will do in us, for us, and with us, all that is pleasing to it.

Considered in themselves, trials certainly cannot be loved, but in their origin, God's will, they are worthy of unlimited love. In Sacred Scripture the Holy Spirit points out that the climax of our Lord's love for us is in the Passion and death He suffered for our sake. To love suffering and affliction out of love for God is the summit of most holy charity since there is nothing pleasant in it, except the divine will. Good things are willingly accepted from God by all; but this acceptance of evil things belongs only to perfect love.

Amid consolations we ought to fear making a wrong

turn by loving the consolation instead of God's good pleasure. A traveler who is not sure of the right road walks on in doubt. The man who is certain of his route goes along cheerfully, confidently, and quickly. Similarly, in a time of affliction we walk with assurance, straight to God's will.

The indifferent heart is like a ball of wax in God's hands, ready to receive all the impressions of His good pleasure. It is a heart equally ready for all things. It does not place its love in the things God wills, but in the will of God Who wills them. The indifferent heart is led on by God's will and wherever His will goes, the soul follows. Such a heart, by a complete surrender of all its affections to God's good pleasure, renders Him a profound obedience of love, uniting itself to His divine intentions everywhere and forever.

Chapter 10

ST. PAUL'S EXHORTATION

ST. PAUL'S WONDERFUL EXHORTATION TO AN ECSTATIC LIFE, LIVED ABOVE NATURE[43]

St. Paul says: "The charity of Christ presses us." (2 Cor. 5:14) Nothing urges someone's heart as much as love. If we know we are loved, no matter by whom, we are impelled to love in turn. We know that Jesus Christ, true and eternal God, has loved us even so far as to will to suffer death on a cross for us. What follows from this? I think I hear St. Paul cry into our hearts' ears, "Christians, it follows that in dying for us Jesus Christ has desired us, that they who are alive may no longer live for themselves, but for Him Who died for them and rose again." How powerful a conclusion is this in matters of love! That is, we should consecrate every moment of our life to the divine love of our Savior. To His glory we must bring all our works, thoughts and affections. Behold the Redeemer stretched upon the cross, dying a death more loving than love itself. If we have a generous spirit, we must say: *I will die with Him, I will burn within the flames of His love.*

The holy ecstasy of true love is accomplished when we live no longer according to human reason and inclinations but above them according to the inspirations and promptings of the Savior of our souls, to whom we sing eternally:

"LIVE ✝ JESUS"!

NOTES

IN THE MIDST OF THE WORLD

In the sections called *Selections from the Saint,* I have chosen to paraphrase much of the Saint's thought, hoping to simplify the writings for the purposes of this book. The following notes are offered so that the Reader may refer to the original sections of the writings of St. Francis de Sales.

INTRODUCTION

JACOB'S LADDER
1. See *Introduction to a Devout Life,* "On the Propriety and Excellence of Devotion".

PART I

CHAPTER 1 - FAITHFULNESS IN ALL THINGS
2. See *Treatise on the Love of God,* Book 12, Chapter 9.
3. See *Introduction to a Devout Life,* "We Must Be Faithful to Both Great and Little Tasks".
   See *Treatise on the Love of God,* Book 12, Chapter 7.

CHAPTER 2 - PRAYER
4. See *Introduction to a Devout Life,* "The Necessity of Prayer".
5. *Ibid.,* "A Short Method of Meditation and First of the Presence of God".

CHAPTER 3 - PRAYER OF THE HEART THROUGHOUT THE DAY
6. See *Introduction to a Devout Life,* "How We Should Receive Inspirations".
7. *Ibid.,* "How We Should Receive Inspirations".
8. *Ibid.,* "Spiritual Retreat".
9. *Ibid.,* "Aspirations, Ejaculatory Prayers, Good Thoughts".

130

CHAPTER 4 - SACRAMENTS AND THE WORD OF GOD
10. See *Directorium nach Franz von Sales,* Oblates of SFS, Austria.
11. See *Introduction to a Devout Life,* "How to Attend Holy Mass"
12. *Ibid.,* "How We Must Hear the Word of God".

CHAPTER 5 - LIFE IN THE PRESENCE OF GOD
13. See *Introduction to a Devout Life,* "We Must Watch Our Affairs Carefully, But Without Eagerness and Solicitude".
14. *Ibid.,* "We Must Be Faithful to Both Great and Little Tasks".
15. See *Spiritual Conferences,* "On Cordiality".
16. *Ibid.,* "On Simplicity".
17. See *St. Francis de Sales in His Letters,* "Crosses".
18. See *Directorium nach Franz von Sales,* Oblates of SFS, Austria
19. See *Spiritual Conferences,* "On Simplicity".
20. See *Treatise on the Love of God,* Book 10, Chapter 14.

CHAPTER 6 - CALVARY
21. See *Directorium nach Franz von Sales,* Oblates of SFS, Austria.
22. See *Treatise on the Love of God,* Book 12, Chapter 13.

PART II

CHAPTER 7 - GOD'S ACTION UPON US
23. See *Introduction to a Devout Life,* "Need of a Guide for Beginning Devotion and Making Progress in It."
24. *Ibid.,* Excerpts from "A Short Method of Meditation".
25. See *Treatise on the Love of God,* Book 6, Chapters 3 and 6.
26. *Ibid.,* Book 6, Chapters 7 to 11.

CHAPTER 8 - OUR COOPERATION WITH GOD'S ACTION
27. See *Introduction to a Devout Life,* "The Choice We Must Make in the Exercise of Virtues".
28. *Ibid.,* "Patience".
29. *Ibid.,* "Outward Humility; Deeper Interior Humility".
30. *Ibid.,* "Meekness Toward Our Neighbor and Remedies for Anger".
31. *Ibid.,* "Obedience".
32. *Ibid.,* "Necessity of Chastity; Advice on How to Preserve Chastity".

CHAPTER 8 - Cont'd.

33. *Ibid.,* "Poverty of Spirit to Be Observed in the Midst of Riches; How to Practice Genuine Poverty Although Really Rich; How to Practice Richness of Spirit in Real Poverty".
34. See *Spiritual Conferences,* "On Simplicity".

CHAPTER 9 - COUNSELS

35. See *Introduction to a Devout Life,* "The Nature of Temptation; Encouragement for a Soul Under Temptation".
36. *Ibid.,* "Anxiety".
37. *Ibid.,* "Sorrow".
38. *Ibid.,* "Concerning Spiritual and Sensible Consolation".
39. *Ibid.,* "Spiritual Dryness".
40. *Ibid.,* "On Desires".
41. See *Spiritual Conferences,* "The Will of God".
42. See *Treatise on the Love of God,* Book 9, Chapters 1, 2, 4.

CHAPTER 10 - ST. PAUL'S EXHORTATION TO AN ECSTATIC LIFE

43. See *Treatise on the Love of God,* Book 7, Chapter 8.

$4.50

IN THE MIDST OF THE WORLD presents a complete guide to holiness in the simple, but sublime, spirituality of **St. Francis de Sales.** Prominent in this work, the reader finds the **SPIRITUAL DIRECTORY** of our Saint a most timely contribution and directive which leads to holiness of life. Following this way will become the means of taking up the challenge and mandate of **Vatican II,** as expressed in the Document, **LUMEN GENTIUM, #40:**

> It is evident to everyone that **all the faithful of Christ, of whatever rank or status, are called to the fullness of the Christian life** and the perfection of charity. By this holiness a more human way of life is promoted, even in this earthly society.

May the message of **IN THE MIDST OF THE WORLD - A Call to Holiness** - inspire many to meet this challenge in their lives!

Additional copies of this book may be obtained from:

SISTERS OF THE VISITATION
Ridge Boulevard at 89th Street   Brooklyn, NY 11209